One New York Man's Journey To Off Grid Living In Montana

By Rich Scheben

Printed in the United States
First printing 2013

A big thank you to my girlfriend Karen for putting up with my writing. Karen was also one of my proof readers as well, which wasn't an easy task since I have never written anything larger than a book report in my life.

A special thanks to the rest of my proof readers whose names are Brandon, Kelly, Dottie, KC, Alec, Paul, Russ, Dave, Bev, Marney, Sherry, Mike, Suzanne and Terry.

Table of Contents

Chapter 10: *Gardening*
We grow our own produce with "raised bed gardening". I explain how to build inexpensive green houses and which vegetables to grow and how and why. Soil, composting, nutrition are also discussed

Chapter 11: *Health/Immune system*
Discussing how to eat healthy and build your immune system. I talk about curing and preventing cancer and the facade that surrounds this money hungry health care system. I use all objective facts and statistics

Chapter 12: *Hobby Farm Animals*
Discussing which animals I chose and the benefits of each

Chapter 13: *Alternative power/energy tips*
Discuss the tools a person would need to start their own solar array or energy set-up. I discuss the fiscal benefits as well as some scenarios which would occur if our "grid" went down

Chapter 14: *Edible and Medicinal Plants*
Discuss the benefits and vitamins of specific plants. Plus, all the wild edible berries I have on my place. I share a story of how I reduced enlarged lymph nodes with medicinal plants, which could have been cancer. My grandmother was in a concentration camp for 20 years and survived because she knew how to eat wild edible plants

Chapter 15: *How about this idea?*
I discuss an idea I have to create a self-sufficiency/preparedness school here in America. Some subjects would include: Alternative energy, living off grid, buying land, raising animals, financial counseling (amortization schedules-principle, interest, equity...), hunting and fishing, canning, hand gun defense, edible and medicinal plants, nutrition, gardening and farming etc

Chapter 16: *Some Independent Final Thoughts*
Just have a few final thoughts to make us all think

Preface

---- The first part of this book answers the harder questions of "why", we as middle class Americans need to be more self-sufficient. This combines the financial, economic, social and political reasons which include real factual examples of "why."

---- The second half of this book delves into the "how to" for a more specific plan of action in regards to being more self-sufficient, while at the same time still tying in the "how to" chapters with financial, economic, social and political rationale.

Introduction

First I have to say that I have had many people hound me to write a book, blog, or pound the pages of Facebook on the subject of self-sufficiency and off-grid living. I've even been approached by production companies wanting to make television shows and documentaries about my "off-grid, self-sufficient" lifestyle. It seems that no matter where I go in this country, my lifestyle becomes an immediate and major topic of conversation. My hope is that this book will finally satisfy some of these requests while at the same time giving as much information and insight as possible to you, the curious reader.

I realize that there are almost 500,000 new books published in America every year alone so I am not expecting some miracle. I just hope that a few folks, here and there, can benefit from the possibility of a new lifestyle: life in which they can have a little more control of their own destiny. Plus, writing a book I have to say was on my "bucket list". I hope I can offer some good reasons, examples and evidence, so that the 90% of Americans who live in urban/suburban America can reap some positive changes with a possible new "game plan" for their lives.

I have noticed that there are a lot of "how to self sufficiency" books on the market but, I haven't noticed any books that mention "why" we, as Americans, need to go back to some form of independence. So, as per much feedback, the first half of this book addresses the financial, economic, social and political reasons WHY we, as Americans, need to become more self-sufficient. This book also includes a story that may be motivational to some folks as well as offering some "how to" chapters on specific skill sets which may be mandatory if you want your children to be free.

I bought my little hobby farm back in the year 2000, moved there permanently by the end of 2005, and started living off grid in 2007. I have not stopped having fun since.

My girlfriend, Karen, and I have made my land our hobby. Everything we do revolves around nature, self-sufficiency and excitement. We hunt, fish, trap, garden, keep goats, chickens, turkeys, etc. We have an extensive interest in botany, including mushrooms, berries, edible plants and medicinal plants as well. Our dwelling is a log cabin, completely self sufficient and disconnected from the corporate electric grid. For all intents and purposes, it is an outdoorsman's paradise... I would even say that 98% of our vacations and recreation revolve around food gathering and nature.

We make our own electricity, hunt our own meat or raise it, go fishing, dehydrate foods, grow our own produce and to some people's surprise, we don't even use a freezer. Canning has been our primary means of preserving foods. We have no "traditional" running water, no interior pipes, no water heater, no pressure tank, no dryer and no automatic flushing toilet. We heat the cabin and prepare our meals with an Amish made wood cook stove. In fact, we call our lifestyle "glamping," in other words glamour camping.

There is no doubt in my mind that the strained economic situation in America has created a growing national interest in the kind of self sufficiency that I have always dreamed of. People are pining to hearken back to the days of independent living, and realizing that something is terribly wrong with the way our "modern culture" has turned out.

For example, the purity of our food has become a glaring concern for many Americans. On my hobby farm, we are able to control and oversee most aspects of our diets. We consume very little if any hormones, steroids, or antibiotics. We use no GMO's or pesticides. (GMO foods are genetically modified "man made" changes which are artificially planted into our food's DNA-this is done in the laboratory and not by nature). Exceptions arise when we are eating out, but in general, we are living far healthier than the common person. I'm not bragging about it, America's food consumption habits are just sad and nothing would make me happier than to see a trend of body well-being and health awareness return to this country.

This off-grid life is a stark and mind boggling transition away from my former existence, having been born in Jamaica, Queens and raised in the metropolitan area of New York City. After living there for 26 years, there is an expectation that a man would not uproot as I did, which is probably why my personal story draws so much attention. The problem was that I could never quite pull my mind or my heart away from the outdoors or mother nature. I am thankful for my experience in the Boy Scouts, which introduced me to the sportsman's world, where self reliance and survival knowledge are esteemed. By the time I was nineteen years old, I had made a decision; I would one day trek to the ranges of the Northern Rockies, and become a New York mountain man. (Possibly the last New York mountain man). I would someday plant my feet on 100 acres of Montana country, I would stand at the foot of my own river, and I would embrace a simpler lifestyle.......

To be clear, this goal was in no way an easy one to pin down, and numerous challenges arose the closer I came to realizing my dreams.

I had attempted to become a N.Y.C. fireman in the late '70's. The idea was to retire at 39, take my pension, and live out the rest of my days off-grid in the Northwest. What I did not realize at the time, but soon became quite familiar with, were the detriments of being an average white male in the belly of a society dominated by political correctness and "victim group status".

The first setback came when a women's group in New York sued the city over the hiring practices of the firefighter's brigade. Why? Because the physical test was too hard! As a result, the physical standards were greatly diminished, just to accommodate certain persons who should not have been applying for the job in the first place, putting victims of fire tragedy at further risk. I was physically fit and able at that age (bench pressing over 300 pounds and could easily do over 100 push-ups), yet, there was a "greater" need for a more politically correct firefighting force. I had always assumed that the whole point of having firefighters around was that they were strong enough to handle horrible life threatening events and carry people out alive. Back then I always thought that qualifications trumped political correctness, according to the women of New York, I was wrong.

I ran into the same ridiculous and illogical scenario when I next worked towards a career with the National Forest Service. This was my plan "B" in getting me to Montana. I had attended forestry school in the Adirondack Mountains and sought a position with the National Forest Service. During the initial interview, I was told point blank that they would not hire me because I was white and male. (They aren't so blunt these days). They opted to hire two female applicants straight out of high school with absolutely no forestry experience whatsoever. A person with a minimal employment background in the world of fast food service had a better chance than I did, despite my training. At the time, my mentors told me to get more aggressive and don't give up, so I didn't!

With my primary career goals in question due to the insanity of our progressive cultural nightmare, which has abandoned all reason in the name of a delusional form of equality that simply doesn't exist, I finally opted into the corporate world, and launched my pharmaceutical career in 1982. (I owe this decision to my father who said "get tough and start knocking on doors, get a resume together and put on a suit and tie)." So I did and I started in the drug industry.

During the 90's, I ran up against more social disparagement dealing with spinal health problems (which I will discuss in later chapters) and my company's refusal to allow me to work part time, again, because they told me that job shares were for females only! I have seen all the strange and depraved absurdities our system has to offer. But, I struggled onward…

In, 1986 I handed in the keys to my company car and told my manager, of the pharmaceutical company I was working for, I was going to Montana to pursue my dream. I then graduated with my third college degree, after having moved across country, and delved into the pharmaceutical industry (again) in the Big Sky State. I had to wear a suit and tie, drive a company car and get three degrees to get there, but my point is that if you truly have a dream that you are striving towards, you do what you have to do to make it a reality. Period.

So here I am now, writing to you as a 53 year old man from the beautiful region of N.W. Montana, living my third life. (New York, corporate America, mountain man "wannabee"). I now own 100 acres of varied terrain on a beautiful river surrounded by the most vast National Forests in the U.S. I am sharing my story with you for many reasons. I see too many people of all ages giving up on their dreams and goals and I sense a malaise and despair present in the next generation. I have noticed that the people who have the most regrets in life are those who not only don't "go for it", but also those who have found no balance in life. Especially those people who have very little passion and enthusiasm for their interests and hobbies. Don't forget that no one can buy back their time or health! Time and health equals freedom!

I have NO special skills or talents. Just a little extra tenacity to achieve my humble ambition for an "off-grid, living off the land" kind of life. MAYBE one half of 1% of Americans live this way, conservatively speaking. That being said, I have to point out that we all need to start thinking outside the box, because everything we think we know about America is being aggressively changed or erased. Our heritage, culture, traditions, and everything that has made America great has been compromised.

Financially and economically, most of our books are "cooked". Some of these manipulated numbers include the GDP to debt ratio, unemployment, CPI and inflation, U.S. Dollar value, precious metals, national debt, housing..... In short, every fundamental index is skewed, manipulated or illegitimate! Corruption, especially in politics and the banking world, isn't even being challenged. I have heard people blame ignorance, indifference and apathy.....who can argue with that, right? But, people's greatest fear is of the consequences of being "politically incorrect". This has caused our society to censor itself in the wake of all this criminality. I say this with a sad heart, but it is politically incorrect to tell the truth in America.

I see too many folks losing their IRA's, 401K's, savings, home equity, and even their homes, while at the same time our current administration is talking about nationalizing all retirements. I see wages going way down (except for government and union workers), and retirement dreams lost. I see a middle class that doesn't even know where to invest anymore, wandering in a fog and unable to control their own destiny. I see a police state protecting the corrupt who make the laws. The future for prosperity looks bleak for the average citizen.

Many in the middle class (especially the private sector) have no "plan of action" for the future. Think about this; in 1960, when I was born, there were 150 Million people in this country.....now it's much more than double. Today 90% of Americans live in urban areas rife with dependent residents with no concept of self sufficiency. Only 10% live rurally. Can you imagine if just a small portion of Americans were to pursue a trend of self sufficiency and lived below their means? Would America not be infinitely stronger and better off in the long run?

Think about the positive movement in National GDP if we started reversing the centralization of our society and went back to the country. The advantages would be astounding.

In the meantime, suburban and urban properties are plummeting in value. Especially, commercial properties. Taxes and other costs, which are directly proportional to the size of a house/structure and its proximity to city limits, are skyrocketing. The bigger the house, the higher the insurance and maintenance as well. How crazy is that! You could be living on a fifth of an acre, like I did growing up in N.Y., having no land for gardens, animals, privacy, or recreation, and be paying out the nose for it in turn. In other words, it's getting harder every day to determine your own financial path when living in urban America. At least for the great majority! Do you think generation X and Y have the savings and investment portfolio to buy your house with a profit? Maybe if inflation was to sky-rocket. Very possible but I wouldn't wish for that either.

What if you lose that great high paying job? What if your pension is lost through the bankruptcy of your employer? What if your 401K disappears due to a market crash? What if the government confiscates your retirement plan because they have printed too much money and they are broke? What if our dollar loses all value? All these scenarios, and many more, happen every day in this world.

It's true that the "country life" isn't for everyone, and a high paying career is enough to tie most people down regardless. But, think of it this way, if your job and your financial foundation are not safe, and your environment is not conducive to your own happiness and the happiness of your family, maybe rethinking your current plan is intelligent and appropriate.

Karen and I were watching an online show focused on living off the grid one day, which is now a serious hot topic in the U.S. today, including words like pioneering, homesteading, and self-sufficiency. The show featured a mother of a family who said she did this for her boys because she didn't like the way our schools, media, and our culture in general were feminizing males. Karen and I couldn't have agreed more. The advantages and benefits of walking away from the mainstream system and taking on a less modern but more rewarding and responsible lifestyle are sometimes harder to see, but, they are there. To be sure, once you make the leap, EVERYTHING changes.

I spend a lot of time showing folks how we live, including raised bed gardening, raising farm animals, hunting, fishing, financial counseling, and off grid living overall. I believe it is important to help as many people as you can, whenever you can. We have had hundreds of guests just in the last year alone, advising them on all manners of economic issues and helping them to pursue their goals.

I have found that many men can only think of the city life, night clubs, girls, money, big corporate job, travel, hotels and restaurants, but in the end, this is barely another memory, and I know from experience. I did all that. Every city, hotel and restaurant eventually looked the same to me. Ultimately, those places became boring. Nature is where it's at for me and I couldn't wait to get there! Nature gives you all the variety and adrenaline rushes you will ever need.

This book is an extension of that principle of aid and advancement that I deeply believe in. As you read onwards, you will find musings and warnings on our country's fiscal, political and social issues, affirmative action and quotas, political correctness, "victim groups status", and, of course, instructions on how to build and maintain an off-grid hobby farm. You will see that I have shot political correctness in the head and have adopted a lifestyle of self-sufficiency and frugality. This book addresses not just a life of self-sufficiency, but of personal sacrifices I have made not for money, but for principle. I hope this story brings you some motivation, inspiration, humor, entertainment and increases your probability of achieving whatever your dreams are. I also hope that this book shows you, the urban/suburban reader, that living in the wild's of nature can be a great alternative lifestyle. Most of all, you'll see that I am living a life of exhilaration and unlimited adventure.

Chapter 1: The Off-Grid Dream And The Tenacity To Reach Your Goals

The first and most formidable obstacle to achieving your dream of Off-Grid independence is, in fact, you and your fears. It never fails. When approached by people searching for that new life, a life of tangible sustainability and freedom from the drudgery and shallowness of consumption, obsessed by modern America, the same excuses always arise:

"I don't have the money to pull it off and will never get it…"

"I like the concept but don't want to abandon the comforts of civilization…"

"I wish I didn't have to suffer through all the work that such a project requires in order to reap the benefits…"

"Can I be off-grid but still live close to the mall?"

It's not that many Americans aren't serious about living off-grid, it's just that they have lived most of their lives brainwashed into believing that the ideal way to live is the urban/suburban cartoon we are surrounded by every day. It is hard to imagine and even terrifying for some to consider the prospect of self reliance and so they conjure up numerous rationalizations in their minds. They fabricate countless reasons why they cannot do exactly what they really want to do deep down-break free.

When a man feels that he is a slave to his work, or a slave to his life, more often than not it is because he has enslaved himself. His excuses become his shackles.

When I was young I lived two lives. The first was the mainstream accepted persona of the New York businessman and night-life denizen. I frequented night clubs, danced all night, and lived for the party. It was the kind of routine that was generally expected of people in the city and in many ways I did enjoy it. However, I was also acutely aware of particular troubles that were escalating within this country and knew, deep down, that the party would one day end for all of us.

My second life was spent in the world of the outdoors. I reveled in the fishing and hunting sports and the paths far away from mainstream America. In fact, I would often find myself caught in a kind of 'Dr. Jekyll and Mr. Hyde' dual existence in which I buried myself in nightclubs during the evenings and climbed out towards the wilderness to go fishing in the mornings. Eventually, I started to realize that the city life was not for me, that there was no substance to it, and that I needed to choose which direction I was to pursue for the future. I chose the woods and the mountains and sought to leave the concrete/asphalt jungle behind me.

I can remember back in the 60's and early 70's watching 'Wild World Of Sports' on TV, with Kurt Gowdy going hunting and fishing in the Rocky Mountains. I remember as a young boy catching snakes and selling them to pet shops. I had landscaping jobs mowing and raking lawns, tending vegetable gardens, and other yard duties. I would walk through the woods, on the peripheries of a golf course about a mile from home and find golf balls on the ground hidden in the leaves and branches. I would then sell those golf balls back to the golfers from the age of 8. (I remember because I recall a golfer asking me how old I was and me telling him that I was 8 years old). Times were different then!

The life of the subsistence landowner was something that appealed to me from very early on. At age 19 it first struck me that I would like to one day to end up in Montana and live off the land. I specifically remember telling people that I wanted 100 acres with a river running through it. I wanted to hunt and fish my butt off, all without corporate electricity or city water or the constant one hundred percent dependance on shopping centers and grocery stores. Some of my family and friends, on the other hand, thought this lifestyle was too rugged and my dreams were just that…........dreams!

I approached the off-grid life and the required relocation from New York to Montana as an adventure instead of a headache and a hassle. It was a mountain to be climbed and conquered. When you are confronted with any struggle, you must ask yourself if the benefits far outweigh the costs. If the answer is yes, as it was for me and off-grid living, then nothing should be able to stop you. There should be no excuses. What our family thinks, what our friends think, even sometimes what our spouse thinks, is irrelevant in comparison to the ultimate success of an honorable dream. Of course, I still had to wait for the right time.

In the meantime, I explained to my skeptical relatives and friends that our country was changing. Taxes and insurance rates were skyrocketing. Inflation of necessities would one day be crippling. America's population centers were too condensed, inefficient, and desperately dependent on the flawed system for their survival. Urban infrastructure would be too expensive to maintain........... I told them that the next generation would be unable to afford houses and other amenities that we had come to take for granted. Or at least the next generations would look at their property tax bill and realize their house was not a good investment. Living in a position of self determination and independence was the only solution for those who did not want to be crushed under the weight of the coming collapse. Unfortunately, I was right.

Today, we see countless crises within the American financial system and all across the globe. The idea of home ownership and subsistence has been perverted beyond all recognition. The "McMansion" empire is crumbling. The banking sector is utterly insolvent and credit markets are freezing up more and more with each passing quarter. The dollar is being printed by our central bank with wild abandon in an effort to kick the can down the road for just a few more years; but honestly, I doubt we have that long.

With the devaluation and inevitable death of the dollar, there will be nothing left but what you can hold in your hands and for most Americans, that's not much.

Therefore, off-grid living is not just healthier but also a more grounded way to live from day to day. It also becomes the common man's strategy for fighting back against a disaster he otherwise has little control over. By taking our fate into our own hands, we insulate ourselves from the trespasses and catastrophes caused by others. The dream is about survival as much as it is about a change in environmental circumstances. The true dangers for the middle class and the poor is when the ratio between humans and natural resources are too high. It is then that true quality of life is lost.

I say this to illustrate the gravity of the situation we are all in and to give some of you out there a reality check as far as what you let get in your way. Most obstacles are miniscule in comparison to the greater threats of financial slavery and loss of savings that you might suffer through if you do not succeed in your off-grid goals. (By the way, when I say "off-grid" I also mean just becoming more self-sufficient.)

Money is always the first issue to arise. The problem is that so many people only consider the initial expenditures involved when diving into this new life but never take into account the extreme SAVINGS involved after they have settled in. My daily costs are limited. My land provides nearly every essential imaginable resource and the financial drain after setting up shop is minute in comparison to that of the average suburbanite. Ultimately, it is about providing for yourself for next to nothing what you once had to pay out the nose for!

I worked multiple jobs and been stonewalled in several careers while building up to my transition into off-grid homesteading. I never had a problem with a person of any race or gender receiving a job that they actually earned and were able-bodied enough to do. But soon, highly qualified individuals (especially if they were white and male) were being shooed away like flies during the application process in many jobs (especially government jobs). They were cast aside and replaced with far less qualified individuals in order to appease the victim groups and their cadres of soul-sucking vampire lawyers. The U.S. was becoming a hive of half–brained bureaucrats and substandard labor drones. The bar was being drastically lowered in terms of quality and expectation, just so certain people with inferiority complexes could feel as though they had accomplished something. All that they had accomplished was to diminish the legitimate productivity and accountability that were vital to the health of our nation.

Let me put this another way. Imagine that you are in college. You're not necessarily fond of it, but you still work hard and study and at the end of your senior year you graduate with your degree. You have put energy into something. You have put sweat and tears into something and naturally you expect that there will be fair returns for your labor. But one day, out of the blue, the school decides that certain people should not have to work as hard as you to get the same returns. The school also decides that some people don't even have to qualify out of high school or pay the same amount of tuition. In fact, they decide that these people should even get the same returns that you worked for!

Ultimately, where do you think the quality of the student coming out of these schools is going to go? Down the crapper, that's where. It's obvious all across the country.

A nation is no different. We now live in a culture which actually rewards mediocrity and oppresses accomplishment. Such a system will one day implode. It is inevitable. This is why the "powers that be" are beefing up the police state, so they can protect their own asses.

This is why the off-grid concept is so important. In the world of off-grid homesteading, there can be no rewards without equal efforts. The off-grid life does not make exceptions for one person over another just because the government identifies them as "special". Nature does not care if you think you are a victim or not. You work hard, or you fail.

The beauty of off-grid life is that it brings TRUE equality to a society. Everyone faces the same problems, and everyone is given a chance to solve these problems. Either they do, or they do not. Their success depends upon how badly they want to succeed, and nothing more.

I believe there will come a time, very soon, where the facade of the "victim group status" theater will come crashing down and all of us, whether we like it or not, we will all be held to the same standards of survival. Many, I suspect, will be found wanting...

Fears of distance from mainstream society are another problem. There are many misconceptions about this. Going off-grid does not necessarily mean abandoning technology. I use LED's, CFL light bulbs and Nokero solar lights. I have a radio (a 1970's boombox) and listen to Sirius radio. I surf the internet and keep up with news events instead of isolating myself in the backwoods from the concerns of the world. I ride a UTV back and forth across my land, not horses (though horses are great if you can keep them). There is a serious delusion out there that going off-grid or living through a collapse will automatically necessitate a return to a pre-industrial 18th century type of existence. This is simply not so. The technological advances of today should be mixed and melded with the agricultural skills of yesterday. Neither should be hastily cast aside if we are to find balance once again in nature and our culture.

By the time I moved to Montana to search for my off-grid land, I had been through a swarm of disappointments, and soon discovered my own physical health was turning on me. A trip to the doctor revealed that I was stricken with two types of spinal stenosis; a loss of cartilage and a collapse in the spinal column that results in damage to the nervous system.

My ability to do strenuous activities was diminished but I did not try to use the ailment as an excuse to give up on my goals and dreams. I carried on and built my homestead. I did hire builders and other workers to erect my structures because I cannot do anything too physical.

I had set requirements in my mind in a very disciplined fashion, which is absolutely crucial if you plan to get anywhere in the field of off-grid living. Know exactly what you want. Understand the steps needed to finish the process. Don't cut corners, and don't become apathetic.

My dream was 100 acres of prime Montana land with a stream and varied topography to offer privacy and variation in my environment. I went through the motions, some of them tedious, in order to research every aspect thoroughly. I had to choose the region where I would build. I had to take into account the average temperatures and elevation. I had to make sure the land was usable for growing and harvesting. I had to ensure rainfall levels would be adequate to nurture the growth of crops, animals, and myself. I had to choose an efficient dwelling which provided space but was easy to heat or cool depending on the season. I had to plan the logistics of water, sewer, electricity (solar) and a generator, as well as fencing, not just to keep my critters in, but to keep wild critters out!

It all seems quite daunting when you make this list in your mind, but taken step by step, your plan will come together. Guaranteed. Persistence, tenacity, and discipline are the key.

Each off-grid homesteader has a tale to tell. I often think of the movie "Rudy", which is about the true story of a young man who dreamed of not only going to college at Notre Dame, but also of playing football there. Faced with incredible odds and everyone he cared about against him, he did exactly what he set out to do. His accomplishment was due to his indomitable will. I loved the part where he said "I can do it coach" when he was trying out for the team (the prep team). Every off-grid dreamer must have this same will, or it will all be for naught. Having a "Someday I'll" attitude is a recipe for failure.

It is, indeed, important to remain realistic, not pessimistic and self defeating. Even with my spinal ailment, I try to learn and adapt everyday using moderation and modifications as a motto. I never considered myself a handyman, and yet today I repair and build much of what I need to survive on the homestead. I adapted, and grew as a person. The off-grid life demands it.

In the second half of this book, we will discuss some of the steps needed to make your dream a reality. The nuts and bolts details, ranging from choosing a region and a building site, to picking a home design, to deciding on livestock and food production methods, and more. But, while the goods and expenses involved in going off-grid are incredibly important, I want you as the reader and prospective homesteader to remember that your mindset is what really matters in all that you do here. Without the right mindset and adventurous spirit, you might as well give up now and save yourself the heartache. Without the will to be independent and self reliant from the system, no matter the effort required, you will not join the ranks of the off-grid pillars of America. Put your mind and heart onto this path fully and anything is possible.

Your loved ones might call you crazy. Your job situation may be chaining you down. You might believe you have "obligations" that make the transition impossible. Forget about all that. Spend less energy worrying about what stands in your way, and more energy figuring out how to do it.

I can honestly say that as I moved off-grid, my life became simpler and more crystalline, not more complicated. It is amazing how many stresses we carry with us in the day-to-day grind of mainstream society that are, in the end, meaningless. The greatest benefit of all in going off-grid is the astonishing clarity that it brings. I ask you now to come with me on this fantastic odyssey, let the absurdities of so called modern life fall away, and view things through a window that most people never get to see. A window into real, organic, dirt under your finger nails freedom…

Chapter 2: Political Correctness "out of control"

I was hired in 1989 by Glaxo pharmaceuticals who by the end of my career with this company in 2001, was known as Glaxo Smith Kline (GSK) pharmaceuticals. By 1994 I was starting to have serious physical problems with my spine, especially my lumbar spine. Driving caused me great discomfort, and it was something I had to do on a regular basis as a pharmaceutical rep in Montana. Pain shot down my legs and into my feet resulting in burning and stinging sensations. Soon I had to make difficult sacrifices, including cutting my regular hunting trips (a love that for me is hard to live without).

In approximately 1997, I was having similar symptoms with my cervical spine and arms. I was starting to have muscular atrophy in my arms and upper body. Even though I tried to continue exercising I could not keep up with the atrophy and shooting pains running down my arms into my hands. I remember going to district meetings where a very kind woman with a nursing background pressed on my back so I could tolerate sitting for long periods. I wish I could remember her name; if she ever reads this book, I just want to say thank you very much for trying to help me.

The Fleet Department (the department which gives out company cars) at GSK told me that I had to stop ruining the drivers seat. Apparently, I was squirming around so much, due to the pain, that I had broken car seats in at least two vehicles while driving. At this time I was really getting concerned and did not know what to do.

Eventually, I obtained a letter from an orthopedic surgeon stating my poor spinal condition. He recommended that I have my driving reduced by 50% immediately or I was going to get progressively worse and suffer long term consequences. I went through the "proper channels" within GSK in order to get some relief while still trying to retain my career.

My requests for a part-time/job share were denied. My managers told me to stop asking for reduced work hours, despite my years of service and my exemplary record with the company. I even had the number one market share in the country for one of the products I had launched. So, I started speaking with attorneys and received an education.

From this point on through the remainder of my pharmaceutical career, I probably consulted with at least 30 lawyers, who warned me to be really careful because GSK was trying to push me to report to "health services". Health Services provides in-house medical evaluations from the company, and usually these evaluations are deliberately designed to protect GSK from a lawsuit. If I submitted to examination, I could be forced out of my job, at only 37 years of age, and placed in a sophisticated database which would hold record of my spinal ailment and prevent me from having proper health insurance or even employment for the rest of my life!

Because my requests, for reduced hours, were continually denied I decided not to use proper channels anymore. Not only my health, but my job and future career were in jeopardy. I continued to make a pretty big "stink" about getting a part-time/job share, but to no avail. Managers from inside and outside of my department who I rarely even spoke with began telling me (off the record) that I needed to stop asking for a job share. I had my suspicions as to what was going on, but had to confirm them through personal investigations.

I spoke to a human resource representative off the record. As it turned out my fears were no conspiracy theory just part of the affirmative action/quota/political correctness of corporate America these days. In other words, I was told that "part-time job shares" were for women ONLY. As it turned out there were no male job shares at that time. Knowing now about the ethics of this company I'm sure they have "cooked the books" by now. It's hard to believe that a company whose "mission statement" is to help people and maintain good health was doing this to me because I was male. If helping people with health problems doesn't mean anything then what the hell are we all doing here? What's it all about? Is this company only about the money? Right then and there I woke up from naivete and unfortunately, I learned the hard way because I've lost approximately 90% of my strength in my arms and upper body.

Believing that America was built on hard work, effort, proven results, qualifications, word of honor, principle, diligence and tenacity, I continued with my requests, and despite the pain, kept working hard. My numbers were excellent and I had the awards to prove it: everything from Representative Of The Quarter to President's Club and many in between. I worked meetings, conventions, and hospital exhibits, standing and sitting in one place for hours enduring agonizing reactions from my spine and extremities. Sometimes my hands shook violently and I had to cross my arms or put them in my pockets so nobody would find out. I often drove while taking painkillers with tears running down my cheeks because I was in so much pain. This happened several times in front of my supervisors and I even begged them to help me drive on some occasions. I knew that if anybody found out I was taking pain killers I would probably lose my job. Thank God GSK didn't make me take any drug tests for painkillers because I would've been out of a career way earlier.

By 2000 I was losing weight drastically. From 1997 to 2000 I lost about 25 pounds..........purely from muscular atrophy. My muscle weight was melting off me like an ice cream cone in July. Though under constant pressure, I continued to refuse to submit to a GSK health examination. I figured I would continue until they fired me, or they allowed me to become the first male to receive a part time job share. I believe that principle should matter in America! It sure didn't mean anything to GSK!

GSK, was doing everything in their power to get me to quit and I even received threats from my manager. Things were getting ugly. I agreed for GSK to pay for an outside medical evaluation from an occupational medical physician, and not surprisingly, she also recommended a 50% reduction in my driving. But to no avail. GSK's actions showed that they would prefer to see my spine deteriorate, me quit, be killed in a car accident or fired rather than give me a part time/job share. All because of political correctness.

Let me put it in perspective for you. Can you imagine human resources telling a woman that she couldn't have an opportunity for a job slot and had to increase the risks to her health because she is female? I wasn't even looking for a promotion, I was actually requesting a demotion, which makes GSK look even more foolish! I just wanted to keep my job/ career! As one attorney told me, if I were female and treated the same way, I would be on the five o'clock news with a $10 million settlement before the end of the day. He even told me that "white males don't have enough "group self pity points". "Group self pity points" ? Really? That was a new one for me............ haven't heard that before! Is this how low America has stooped? I wonder if the government is going to start referring to these pathetic insults to women and minorities as "GSPP syndrome." Just remember, every new syndrome or addiction creates a new synthetic drug and new government department including new employees to "monitor things". What a racket!

Listen for it on the "old media" we should start hearing it sometime by the end of 2013. So, I asked this attorney to take my case on a contingency for me and fight this ridiculousness. He said the odds of success for a white male is "a thousand to one regarding reverse discrimination". Plus he said that his practice over the last 20 years was mostly from woman successfully suing men at an eight to one ratio. He told me that he wasn't going to buck the system because he was laughing all the way to the bank. I remember he owned property down in Central America and was planning on getting out of America to retire before things got "too bad". That figures!

Finally, I received a job offer from Merck, which included working on a product line that competed directly with Glaxo (a small bit of justice.) Plus I became the very first male in their company with a part time/job share. Just to be clear, I was told the only reason that I could get this job share was because my job share partner was a female. Figures! I was initially hired by a male manager and he was a GREAT person with an excellent work ethic. I owe a three year extension of my career to him. He was a man with great honor.

I continued to hide my spinal ailment in order to avoid the dangers of "liability paranoia" that are so pervasive in corporate America today. I was able to hold off Merck for a while, but not forever.

By the time I was 44, I was finally forced into visiting the company's "health services" department. My attorneys related that they were surprised I had been able to go so long without being required to get these objective medical tests. At least by this time I wasn't in my 30's, meaning I had avoided the bullet long enough to build some savings and a life. In other words, I was able to extend my career by about 7 years by "dodging" these objective medical tests the last two company's wanted to give me. I like to call it the "corporate liability protocol". Eventually, I couldn't come up with any more excuses for not taking these tests. Too many people were telling me that I looked like I was in a lot of pain. Merck was forcing me to go to "health services", quit or go full time......... the gig was up! Even my attorneys were telling me that I could be sued because I was not telling the company how much pain I was in, how little sleep I was getting, and that I was on some prescribed PRN painkillers. (PRN means "as needed"). I eventually was given an MRI and an EMG (a nerve conduction test), and of course, my secret was discovered. I had two types of spinal stenosis along with nerve damage in my arms, herniated and ruptured discs and muscular atrophy down my arms and into my shoulder, pecks and lats. My neurologist told Karen and myself to "run, not walk, to the nearest neurosurgeon". Basically, my cervical spinal canal was caving-in. There are no words to describe the pain I live with every day in my spine, arms and still sometimes my legs.

Merck told me to drive my company car home immediately. I was done, in other words force-ably retired. Despite graduating from three colleges and having 20 plus years of pharmaceutical experience, my career was over. My attorneys said that no one would ever hire me again with a spinal condition of such magnitude. I knew it was coming…it was only a matter of time.

Some might ask why didn't I go on disability 7 years earlier when GSK was trying to force me to go to "health services" and take medical tests? Well, I was making a good salary along with multiple benefits including a company vehicle; disability would have utterly destroyed my financial future. (Basically, disability is "beer money"). Ultimately, I suffered through those extra years to ensure that I would have something tangible by the time my spinal condition was discovered. Besides, principle mattered to me and I wouldn't give up until I was the first male job share for some company! I know one thing for sure, if GSK would have given me a job share when I initially asked for it, my health would be 1000 times better than it is today. All that driving has deteriorated my spine.

So, when all this went down I started seeing neurosurgeons and orthopedic surgeons. The local physicians I knew personally told me not to get the surgery in Montana. I did consult with some local neurosurgeons but I wanted other opinions. So I consulted with surgeons from Seattle to Tampa. For the most part, they all told me different things. The most common response from surgeons was "if you have a hundred foot rope and 90 feet of it is frayed, which part am I supposed to repair?" Another popular response was, "I may be able to give some pain relief to your arms but not your spine". One physician even told me that "I had a much higher percentage chance of being paralyzed from my neck down with this surgery than the average person". That was all I had to hear! Because the risks of surgery on my spine are extraordinarily high, I have turned to more natural healing methods. I now use a rife machine, a violet ray machine, a spine Doc, a cervical spine traction unit, an energy cleaner, have occasional laser therapy, one hour of physical therapy per day, consult with Herbalists and Naturopathic Doctors and I try to do as much walking as possible. (As long as it is not on concrete, asphalt or anything hard.) I have not given up on my health or my future even though my arms and hands often feel like they are going to break from the pain plus, it feels like father time has poured gravel down my spinal canal. I just do as much as I can with moderation and a lots of modification. In fact, I am finally (sometimes) just starting to feel a little better......as long as I don't overdo it.

I am relating my personal situation to you not to complain about my challenges, but to show you that I understand very well what it's like to suffer great difficulties and hardships while trying to accomplish a dream.

I became a lot less naive at this point in my life, and my eyes were opened to a darker side that some people often ignore. I realized that the companies I worked for were not helpful or vital to the health of our society. Big Pharma was not paid to prevent or cure disease but, in fact was profiting from the management of the symptoms of diseases.

It's funny but as I write this chapter, there have been some very damaging headlines on the pharmaceutical industry. Headlines like: "Big Pharma Criminality No longer A Conspiracy Theory Bribery, Fraud, Price-Fixing Now A Matter Of Public Record." We are now seeing Glaxo Smith Kline pleading guilty to bribery, fraud, and other crimes. According to US federal investigators, Glaxo has been routinely bribing doctors with luxury vacations and paid speaking gigs, while fabricating drug safety data and lying to the FDA. They have been caught defrauding Medicare and Medicaid out of billions of dollars. GSK has also deceived regulators about the effectiveness of their drugs. They have relied on these deceptive practices to earn billions of dollars while intentionally selling dangerous medications to unsuspecting consumers and medical patients. But for all the exposure, this is only a small part of what they have been doing. In fact, I just heard on the news that they are pulling off the same crap in China. They are not satisfied with lying, bribery and fraud with the American people and destroying peoples health but now these greedy bastards are trying to start WWIII. I hope China calls me as a witness to testify against GSK.

GSK doesn't deny any of it. The company just pays multi-billion dollar fines, apologizes to their customers, and then continues conducting business as usual.

If Big Pharma would falsify data on vaccines and other drugs what else would the industry do? Would they falsify efficacy data on other prescription drugs? Would they exploit children for deadly vaccine trials? Would they invent fictitious diseases to sell more drugs? Would they unleash bio weapons to cause a profitable pandemic? Would they conspire with the CDC to spread fear to promote vaccinations? Would they silence whistleblowers who try to go public with the truth? Would they give people cancer via viruses in vaccines? Would they destroy the careers of scientists who question big Pharma? Would they force a medical monopoly on the entire US population via socialist health care legislation? These questions should be looked at by you the consumer. Anyone reading this who has kids, grand kids or elderly parents should be greatly concerned.

I remember, during a GSK meeting, I suggested introducing a nutritional care program for patients in America. I remember being looked at by management like some alien from outer space. The managers said nothing because they knew that profits were more important...........I'm sure that little incident didn't help my career!

I learned about Glaxo Smith Kline's unethical practices too late in my life, and unfortunately, it's not just Glaxo. Merck also has "blood on their hands." I am reading now that Merck has falsified vaccine data, spiked blood samples, and more according to former employees. Former Merck virologists, say the company falsified test data to fabricate a vaccine efficacy rate of 95% or higher. They spiked the blood tests with animal antibodies in order to artificially inflate the appearance of immune system antibodies. Merck pressured these individuals to participate in the fraud and subsequent cover-up. The falsified trial results were used to swindle the US government out of hundreds of millions of dollars for a vaccine that does not provide adequate immunization. They even intimidated scientists with threats of imprisonment unless they remained silent.

Other headlines read:

"Merck's Mumps Viral Strain Is 45 Years Old"

"Complete Medical Farce Regarding Merck's Vaccines"

"Merck fraudulently misrepresented the efficacy of its vaccine and contributed to the spread of infectious disease, says lawsuit..."

Everything mentioned above regarding Glaxo and Merck is PUBLISHED DATA in the public domain.

Some of these crimes against the American consumer are now out in the open, and not a single CEO or executive have been prosecuted. Not one. International drug companies are above the law just like the Mafia bosses of earlier eras, and they are corporate monopolies endorsed by our government with little to fear. Just think, if you as an individual went around town bribing doctors, falsifying data, selling a fraudulent product to the government, lying to regulators, engaging in anti-trade price-fixing and threatening your employees into silence. What would happen to you? Do you think you would go to prison? Of course it's a rhetorical question. You would be rotting in prison for the rest of your life. These companies slip through the fingers of justice because our system is engineered to reward institutionalized corruption, not punish it. Criminality along with political correctness has trumped every aspect in America that made us great. This same political correctness has skewed every principle we used to hold dear in this country. It has poisoned us against ourselves.

What if health care was based on your skin color, gender, wealth, ideology and philosophy? What if you just got jobs, health care opportunities and benefits based on just agreeing in public conversation with the "right people"; even if the masses saw this as brown nosing and blowing smoke up everyone's ass? (The "right people" being the government and the wealthy who control our media and oligarchy's). What if principle no longer mattered? What if you were so afraid to respond publicly to anything that you had to wait for the "politically correct police" to sanction what you could say? What if one day we will all wake up and find that the word "diversity" is only applicable when "the right people" say it for their own benefit!

Months before leaving Merck, I put my house on the market with plans to resign and realize my off-grid goals. I was trying to sell my house so I could skirt these medical tests which would uncover my spinal stenosis and nerve damage. Unfortunately, I couldn't sell my house in time to avoid this terrible news being placed on my health record.

I knew that I would have to prepare well for the future and place myself in a position which would sustain me for the rest of my life regardless of how bad things became in the U.S. or with my health. The establishment has made it more and more difficult for honest men and women to progress or prevail when one gets a diagnosis that is debilitating.

This is why I am so adamant about the off-grid philosophy. I have played the game by the rules and seen how it gets people almost nowhere. The more reliant we as a culture become on the system, the more we are enslaved to live off of "beer money". The only viable option I see available to us is to walk away from it more and more everyday. We must strive for independent living, and relearn how to provide necessities for ourselves, or we will lose everything that makes us human.

We hear excuses all the time. People often complain that they'll never be able to make it work, or that their personal struggles are just too insurmountable. I'm here to tell you that's all garbage. There is ALWAYS a way. The secret is to realize how peripheral and inconsequential our private problems are in the face of our dreams. You can remove obstacles anytime you choose, if you are willing to put in the work, instead of defeating yourself before you even begin. During this scenario with my company and diagnosis/health, I was also going through a divorce and my father was dying of bone cancer.

I went through a lot to finally get my little off-grid "hobby farm", but if I had to do it all over again, I would do it mostly the same way. Even though I knew my health would be greatly compromised, I would still stand up for my principles. I am writing this book at the age of 53. I am using Dragon software so I can speak in a microphone instead of typing on the computer the whole way. I can type with ease for a couple of minutes, after that it's very uncomfortable keeping my arms up to type for long periods of time. I do have some regrets knowing that I have to sell off a piece of land here and there for the majority of my income but, as the old saying goes "you can't take it with you".

However, I feel blessed everyday for my little hobby farm because it gives me the opportunity to live life the way I want, to eat healthy, to be semi-active, and to not be told I can't have this opportunity because I am an American white male.

Chapter 3: The Rise Of Political Correctness And The Fall Of The Middle Class

If you want to find one of the primary root problems for the destruction of the American middle class, all you need to do is look to the cult of political correctness. In fact, an accurate antonym for political correctness these days is the word "truth". Political correctness has become the destructive siren call of our once free-spirited, no-nonsense culture. It has become the pagan god of the modern metro-sexual, consumption-obsessed, progressive socialist ilk. Everything these people know about life they learned from television, and like all socialists, their foremost desire is to ensure that all the rest of us adopt their dogmas and taboos. The majority of the denizens of political correctness abhor Christian observance, claiming that Christianity is an assimilating force, a domineering, archaic, and subjugating institution. And yet, it is they who go out of their way to enforce their taboos on the rest of America. In the end, political correctness is not about the heritage and traditions that built America; it's about social control through imposed etiquette. It's about shaming, bribing, intimidating or threatening other people into conformity. A great example is "sensitivity training". To sum it up simply.............do what I say.............don't tell anyone I said it.............. and your paycheck and pension will keep coming. Forget about right or wrong, principle, hard work, proven results, qualifications........ Forget about everyone on American soil living and abiding by the same rules, laws and having the same accountability.

The truth is not always "nice" or "pleasant". It is not always clean and wholesome and gender conscious. The truth sometimes requires words that have been stricken from our vocabulary as "forbidden". The truth often targets people who are protected by our society with "victim group status". If you point out the flawed nature of this system, or question the double standard which now shields "victim groups" from criticism, get ready to be demonized in every way imaginable. Even if 99% of what you say is true and 1% is ambiguous........they will attack your 1% data in order to discredit you. Are you a public figure with celebrity status? Keep your mouth shut, otherwise, they'll add you to a list of monsters along with Hitler and Stalin. Even when speaking about TRUE stories, you will be labeled with "controversial, confrontational, angry/bitter, bigot, racist, sexist, misogynist, cynic, hater, homophobe, white supremacist, radical, extremist, asshole, conspiracy theorist" or any other name with the word "anti" in front of it will fly liberally, from the mouths of people who want division and not diversity! Of course there are many more names mentioned by Hollywood movies and the "left" but, these are what I call the "dirty dozen" names. (And yes, I know that I named more than a dozen words). These words are mentioned by the "old media" as often as we all hear about "testosterone" and "erectile dysfunction" medication on radio and television advertisements. Most people are afraid to say the truth because of the fear of being singled out and called these names. Most of America has forgotten what it is like to fight for principle.

Forget the labels and let's look at the cold hard facts. The bottom line is, in any economy, when the system gives mass favors to one group over another based on race or gender or extreme wealth or sexual orientation instead of legitimate working experience and ability, that system is going to degrade and eventually fail. This goes for a system that overtly rewards inadequate and inexperienced working white males as well. This is also noticed in too many nepotism situations.

Real free markets, not to mention supply and demand, require productivity and ingenuity, not some abstract and arbitrary idea of "fairness". Race, gender and anything else should have nothing to do with it. One of a million examples I can come up with is high school/college sports. Getting rid of the most popular sports that bring in the most money for the school, just because there aren't the same number of "girls" sports as "boys" sports, is just plain stupid!

For years, people have been blaming America's division and reduction of the middle-class on things like apathy, indifference and ignorance. Even though the above mentioned are part of our demise, the biggest reason for the loss of our middle-class is the fear of the consequences of being politically incorrect. (This is one of the facts I feel the need to be redundant on). In other words, it is politically incorrect to say the truth in America unless you have victim group status or are protected in some way. We all hear that today's youth has a "generational" ideology and philosophy-do they really? Or are they just afraid to say the truth? Do they think that talking in the language of political correctness will give them a job or other opportunities? This atmosphere of dread is slowly killing our ability to function in a prosperous manner.

Government refers to it as "protectionist status", but these are terms that are very rarely used in the mainstream media. Luckily, some conservative and Liberty Movement media sources are gaining ground and telling the situation like it is.

The "powers that be" are working a well oiled plan of division that has been successfully implemented for over thousands of years all over the world. This division prevents the middle class and poor from uniting together. More division......more distractions........less freedom and liberties (for the middle class that is)! The only exceptions most people can see that are increasing in "freedoms" are abortions, sodomy and divorce. So if you're into killing your own baby, kinky sex and are a quitter by nature....life is acceptable! This "system" is meant to keep the "powers that be" wealthy and everyone else in "beer money". You can go back to the Roman Empire and see similar examples by their "elites".

I keep very busy outside, but when I get a chance to listen to the radio I listen to one of my favorite talk radio hosts, Andrew Wilkow of the Wilkow Majority. He has the guts to talk about affirmative action, quotas, "victim group status" and the tools the "powers that be" have used to divide and conquer America. Personally, I think Andrew should run for president. I have also heard Rush Limbaugh speak about affirmative action/quotas on a few occasions. I feel very strongly that we should not be ashamed to discuss these matters in a rational way. The political elite have for too long used the dogmatic shackles of PC Culture to silence us, or dissuade us from asking the right questions. It's also important to note that I do not agree with 100% of what Andrew Wilkow or any conservative talk show host or anchor says. I may agree between 80% and 90% of what they say, but no one agrees with anyone 100%. So, that being said, everyone has a different perspective on ideologies, philosophies and economic strategies. But, at least these people have the guts to say what they think and use objective facts in their arguments.

There are quite a few other good talk show hosts out there on the radio and internet. Some other radio talk show hosts who I agree with most of the time are David Webb and Sean Hannity. There are also a plethora of talk show hosts on the Internet who are very good like "offthegridnews. com" and the John Moore show called "Thelibertyman.com". I will give you a short list of other "on line" news sources that could benefit you in getting the truth regarding economy, finance, health and many other concerns we have in America today. There are a lot more sources to choose from and it's up to you to do the research.

www.dailybell.com   www.naturalnews.com   www.paulcraigroberts. com www.worldnetdaily.com www.larouchepac.com www.stevequayle. com www.survivalblog.com www.theblaze.com www.thelibertycrier. com www.maxkeiser.com www.trendsresearch.com www.infowars.com

Right now in America what we need are people with guts. I'm not saying we don't need brains, strategy and a plan of action but we need guts, desperately. Having guts includes being able to cut through hoity-toity p.c. garbage and get to the bottom of our social difficulties in a plain-spoken way.

There are hundreds, if not thousands, of subsets under the category of political correctness. This division tactic has made the top 2% of America and the world so wealthy that they have conquered the middle-class. These people own over 50% of the world's assets and some believe there is enough evidence to suggest that they are also hiding tens-of-trillions of dollars "off shore". Using political correctness, these powerful elite have the ability to redistribute wealth and jobs based on victim group status, which at first glance appears to be an effort to "help" society, but in reality, it is destroying the overall fabric of our country's fiscal health. Yes, redistribution of wealth makes everyone "equal" by making we in the middle class EQUALLY POOR! All this division takes the eye off the ball so the "powers that be" can screw society as a whole while making themselves richer. Many of the "sheeple" are beginning to pay attention and are realizing that the "Emperor has no clothes"! Can't you all see that the "powers that be" are hurting every group they say they are trying to help?

America is a country that was built by hard work, effort, proven results, qualifications, word of honor, principal, diligence and tenacity. (I hope I'm also redundant on this as well.) Unfortunately, as many attorneys have admitted to me, it is easier to get a job, keep a job, or sue depending on your "victim group status". In other words, if you are a poor or middle-class white male, heterosexual with a Christian background or name, qualifications very rarely matter and your prospects for a job (especially in government) are slimmer compared to your "victim group" counterparts. The top few percent can afford to give their white male sons all the jobs in the world. They have the connections, educational opportunities, money and the nepotism to keep "their own" in wealth for the rest of their lives. Unfortunately, the middle-class has to divvy up what little scraps they have to give to the rest of the people who have victim group status. This is why the poor and middle class white male have been the most discriminated group in the country for the last two generations............but, without any victim group benefits and, I might add, we don't even want it. Just another distraction to keep the rich wealthier. How pathetic has our country become because of the constraints of "political correctness"? As Americans, we should all prefer to be hated for telling the truth than be loved for blowing smoke up someone's ass and telling certain people what they want to hear.

Some Examples of "Victim Group" Status are as follows:

1) I remember a group of firemen in Connecticut that were issuing tests for promotion a few years ago and most, if not all, of the highest test scores were white males. A judge (who now sits on our Supreme Court) had abruptly, canceled the promotions due to a lawsuit. The case was finally taken to the Supreme Court where the national media was forced, at least for a few moments in time, to give attention to the issue. The case exposed the fact that the judge had canceled the promotions because all, or most of those who qualified, were white males. One fireman even had dyslexia and had to hire a private tutor. He still scored high enough on the test to get the promotion, but his promotion was canceled just because he was a white male. Has this country gone insane? I believe they finally received their promotions because of public outrage.

2) Just recently in Missoula, Montana, another crazy stunt was almost successfully pulled off by a homosexual man. Apparently, he faked an attack by alleged "heterosexual white males" and even tried to blame them for his bashed-in bloody face. Thank God, someone caught him on film trying an unsuccessful "flip" in which he landed on his face. So, because of the video evidence this moron received a small fine.

3) A similar story happened a few years earlier, also in Missoula, with a lesbian couple. Apparently, their garage burned down and they blamed "homosexual haters". The fire marshal revealed that they were at fault for the garage burning down.

4) I just heard on the radio yesterday from FOX news about a lesbian couple who recently "broke up". Apparently, the one getting the custody of the child is suing the man who supplied the DONOR sperm for financial support. Hello, America are you a awake?

5) I remember another story, reported on FOX NEWS, a discussion regarding astronomy. Apparently, one of the things that was mentioned was the phenomenon of a "black hole". It turned out that a bunch of black women were threatening a law suit because they thought the person discussing this astronomy phenomenon was talking in a derogatory way about black women. These women should be consulting with honorable black leaders like Dr. James Manning, Bill Cosby, Dr. Ben Carson, Dr. Alveda King and Deneen Boreli. (Look them up).

6) I know of police departments that were looking for in-house promotions for detective..........I bet you guessed this outcome already! A female who was unqualified threatened sexual harassment if she didn't get the job, so the department gave her the job so there wouldn't be "politically incorrect" publicity. The male police officer, who didn't get

the job, even though he was more qualified, just had to grin and bear it..........I bet he wasn't grinning!

These stories are going on and on and on everyday like a broken record, every month, year, decade and generation................on and on and on.................. We are a broken record with a broken country!

7) Another national story broke several years ago. This story, surprisingly, made it into PEOPLE magazine in 2002. A man who thought he was happily married had four kids with his wife and thought everything was normal. Well, it wasn't! Long story short, the wife had a few affairs. It turned out that the husband became suspicious and had his childrens DNA checked. Unfortunately, it turned out to be every father's nightmare. Three out of four of his children were NOT his............... that's right, the husband wasn't the father.

So, as everyone might expect they got a divorce. The judge ordered the husband to pay child support for all four children. (As Bill Cosby would say "come on people"). Another way to look at this is that the wife had no or little accountability or consequences for her actions. To put it another way she had a tiered system of special rules, laws and accountability based on "victim group status". Even though, for generations now, women have had the last "say" regarding having sex or getting married, they don't want to have equal responsibility or accountability. Women have had the ability to say "NO" for sex and marriage for generations now. They make the final choice! There are two kinds of sex regarding this context: first is "adult consensual sex" and the second is "rape". If the female has adult consensual sex, and cheats on her husband, why does she have no accountability or responsibilities? Why should the female get victim group status, be treated like a baby, and the man has to pay for her decisions? Do you think the "powers that be" want synergy or division? Unfortunately, this example I just shared is happening all around the country in almost every state. The ridiculous in America is turning out to be the new normal. What was right is now wrong! Left is now right and up is now down!

8)This next scenario was shared with me from an out of state physician many years ago. This Doctor put himself through medical school and I can tell you that this is a very difficult and expensive endeavor. I have known a lot of physicians since I was in the pharmaceutical business for over 20 years and heard a lot of stories but, this is amongst the worst that I have ever heard regarding "victim group status".

This Doctor bought his dream house prior to his marriage. He eventually was married and had a couple of kids. (I am going to try to make a long story short). One day after working long hours he came home to his wife and she was demanding a divorce. He refused because he gave his oath (word of honor) to God and other witnesses plus, he didn't believe in being a quitter. Since he refused to leave his home, she tried a different approach and contacted a judge and told this judge that "I think my husband is looking at my children the wrong way". At the risk of grossing anyone out this is an obvious implication by the wife that the doctor might want to have sex with his own children. There was no evidence and no proof.................. just her accusation.

So, as you can imagine, the doctor had to finally leave his home that he owned prior to marriage. By this time, he had lost a considerable number of patients because his wife told everyone what an "asshole" he was. About a week or two later, after the doctor had to move out, the wife moved in the "other man"; apparently she was having an affair. (But, that means nothing today because marriage is now "no fault", which means no accountability). Shortly after that, the kids had witnessed, the wife and the "other man" having sex in different rooms around the house. The kids informed the father (doctor) and the father tried to be a man and a good father and do something about it. Immediately, the wife called the cops and the doctor received a restraining order. Right after this the judge threatened the doctor that he would not be able to visit his own children again if the wife complained about him again. In fact, the judge told the doctor that he may only be able to visit his own children with supervision. By this time, the wife had told everyone within the hemisphere about this doctor being such an "asshole" so he had to leave the state to find a new practice.

There are a lot of very sad aspects to the story and unfortunately they keep coming. This Doctor, even though he wasn't the quitter, liar, and did nothing illegal, unethical or immoral, he still had to pay for the mortgage, taxes, insurance, maintenance, child support, alimony and every other bill she could allocate to his accounts payable. I can't imagine the pain this poor man went through. This woman and her boy friend had not worked a job during this whole ordeal and has lived only off of the monies coming in from this physician. I haven't talked to this Doctor for many years but, I can only assume that this woman has not had any legal trouble, with this case, because of her "victim group status".

As "the system" continues to pull "fathers" out of the family, our country will continue to lose its discipline and sense of responsibility. Generally speaking, it has been a socioeconomic fact for decades now, that more responsible people are having fewer or no children while the less responsible are having more.

9) Another example of where we are heading as a country. When I was in a bank just after Christmas. While waiting on line this gentleman asked me if I was here to get some "Monopoly money". It was pretty obvious that he was talking about our fiat currency backed by debt-a debt so large, where our U.S. Treasury is handing out IOU's. Where the Federal Reserve is buying back this debt. (Go ahead and try to pull that one off to your debtors! You will be in jail before you can say.......... why me?)

Anyway, he started talking about affirmative action and quotas just out of the blue. He mentioned that when he walks in to a doctor's office, he asks himself "did that woman or minority earn their job" ? He questioned their competency! I have heard this argument by so many people INCLUDING many females and minorities. It is an insult to them and to America! This conversation occurs all too often especially when walking out of any government building or a large corporate oligarchy.

10) Do you remember Fort Hood? I think it was around November 5th, 2009. Thirteen murdered, thirty-two wounded. An "American" Major killed many of our soldiers on a military base. Apparently, he was saying a lot of derogatory stuff about America's traditions, heritages and culture and was never reprimanded because he was Muslim, as per the media. I remember reading an article that said; if a white male Christian said any of those things he would have been arrested way before this incident happened. Political correctness kills! I wonder what was this officers punishment?

11) This next example of political correctness, specifically victim group status, is one that is very personal to me. I have struggled over whether or not to make these facts public. I have told very, very few people about this experience in my life. I have also felt the need to tell this story to a few friends recently in order to get their opinion regarding its addition to this book. Everyone I told this story to recently has made it adamantly clear that it should be in the book. Since one of the goals of this book is to help reverse the despair of our nation and eliminate political correctness, I feel obligated to share this story. So, long story short, this happened to me when I was about 9 or 10 years old. I remember every detail like it was yesterday.

Apparently, from what many people have told me, my mother has always been very over protective toward my little brother. One day I remember my little brother screaming to my mother that I was teasing him. I remember it well. I wasn't even using words just sounds with my cheek. (Now keep in mind my little brother was like a toddler at this point, since he is 5 ½ years younger than myself). At that point my mother lost her cool and threw a knife at me. I remember pulling the knife out of my arm............. I don't remember what curse words I knew at that age, but I'm sure a few were flying out of my mouth after that knife had embedded in my arm. Before I continue with this story, I have an obligation to mention a few things. First of all, I forgave my mother many years ago. I did everything in my power to lie about this incident to my school and my friends in order to protect my mother from the law and whatever stigma she would have to live with for the rest of her life. I feel that most people deserve a second and sometimes a third chance. I also feel that everyone has a time in their life that they regret. I'm sure this scenario has always wreaked havoc in the back of her mind many times over. As for my brother, he has always been a great little brother and has turned into a wonderful man! In fact, he's a police officer and I'm very proud of him.

Unfortunately, there is no way I can describe the political correct agenda of this story without sharing the last paragraph.

At that point, unable to stop the bleeding, my mother drove us (me and my little brother) to the doctor where she (the physician) sewed up the knife wound. I remember my mother almost hallucinating from panic. I remember my mother begging the doctor not to tell anyone she did this to me. I remember everything like it was yesterday. I remember the pediatrician telling my mother that she wouldn't put this information in my medical records and that she wouldn't tell anyone about this as well. Then I remember, as I was being stitched up, the pediatrician telling my mother "that if you were the father or any other man I would've called the cops on this behavior." (I'm sure I am paraphrasing a little because it was a long time ago and I was just a little kid). Then and there I knew I had to protect my mother from the age of 9 or 10. I know most of you who are reading this example of political correctness may not believe it. But just remember I will always have the scar on my arm to prove it! This was my first personal exposure to victim group status in America.

I never brought that incident up to my mother because I know she has a great heart and is a good person. Before I was 25 years old I was able to send both of my parents to Paris, London, a Caribbean cruise and dozens of Broadway plays. I have to believe that forgiveness trumps despair. I also believe that attitude creates altitude.

I try to laugh and tell jokes everyday. I think we should all laugh and tell jokes and forget about political correctness. It's a shame that so many people who just tell a joke on the job are being fired and sued. The people who are doing the suing are the people with the highest protectionism from victim group status. It's appalling and an insult to all women and minorities. Not to mention Asians. Because they are arguably the most intelligent and hardest working people on the planet. We as Americans should have the same rules, laws and accountability for all.

12) Remember the Travon Martin case a couple of years ago? NBC moved around the audio words of his so called attacker (I think his name was Zimmerman) to make it sound as though he was saying something totally different. NBC has done this several times and just apologizes when they get caught. I remember NBC and others in the "lame stream" media dialing it down a few notches when they found out that Zimmerman was Hispanic. In fact, they started calling him a "white Hispanic". I have even seen cases where the "old media" has hired actors to represent victims being interviewed during certain catastrophes. We are a screwed up country! This is why I get 99% of my news and information off of credible internet news sites.

I often wish we could press a button and get all of our WW ll vets to come alive, at say 30 years old and then these problems would probably all vanish in a couple of months. We have really let our combat veterans down. We have really let America down, especially its middle-class. Remember the Battle of Athens, Tennessee; August 1946. Look it up, it's also a movie! "An American Story".

13) I just heard on the radio that Massachusetts is trying to create a new law for "transgenders" in school. Apparently, now they can use whichever bathroom or locker room they want. They can join any sports team they want-girls or boys. It's up to the discretion of the individual which "gender" they choose to be. So, if a boy puts on a dress and make up he can say he is "transgender" and go into the girls' locker room. No problem! Hello............is anyone home? I guess we have reached the point where nothing matters any more.

When the "powers that be" create special rules, laws and accountability for people that have been "dubbed" victim group status, it can only mean the inevitable death of a great nation.

14) I have just heard on the news a story about a football player. Apparently, he was one of our nations top recruits out of school, and just spent 5 years in jail because a female told authorities that he raped her! Long story short, she just confessed that she lied and this poor guy was finally released from prison. Do you think she will go to jail for 5 years? Does this sound like the same rules, laws and accountability to

you? Do you think this behavior give females more equality or more victim status? Do you think this is a way for the "elite" to place fear in females so they have to look over their shoulder? Are they to be afraid of male retribution? Is this a ploy by the "elite" to encourage the majority of females to vote for a big government and a police state? Will men show less respect and trust for woman and not want to get married? Will more woman have babies out of wedlock? Will there be fewer families raising their own children and making parental decisions? Do men now have to video their sexual encounters with women to prove it's consensual and not rape? Should men only have sex with hookers to erase any ambiguities of adult mutually consensual sex? Does this create more division or synergy in America? I think we all know where this is heading! One day, America's women will wake up and their children will be raised by the "state" and they will have NO say in their up-bringing. Or maybe we will just have Sharia Law?

15) Have you visited any Indian reservations lately? How many Indian treaties have been kept by the Federal Government over the last 200 years? The Federal Government screwed them in the 1800's and continue to do so. (They are even using the Indians to obtain "water rights" so they can push their "agenda 21" propaganda in order to control more people).

When people get retirement benefits from a child it will ruin any culture. Then chemical dependency will go up and life expectancy will drop. How can the Federal Government give all these benefits to "Indians", by putting them on the "rolls" for being only 1/16th Indian? Let me put this into perspective. An American "Indian" can be 1/16th Indian, 1/16th Irish, 1/16th Russian, 1/16th German, 1/16th Swedish, 1/16th English, 1/16th Mongolian, 1/16th Polish, 1/16th Canadian, 1/16th Mexican, 1/16th Australian, 1/16th Scottish, 1/16th Chinese, 1/16 Japanese, 1/16th Romanian, 1/16th Greek AND still be considered "Indian" on a lot of reservations. (When this example is printed out, does it not look ridiculous? Hello!) This means he can get on the "rolls", can live on the reservation and receive every benefit in the book (but at the lowest levels). Of course life expectancy and quality of life will be a lot less. This is so ridiculous that you have to ask yourself, is this being done for the "Indians" or for the Federal workers' paychecks, pensions and job security?

Take out of the "kitty" only if you put into the "kitty". Remember the saying "Give a man a fish and you'll feed him for a day. Teach a man to fish and you'll feed him forever?" Social security is a great example. If you were forced or volunteered to pay into that fund, you have a right to take that money. The same for workmans comp. It's not an entitlement when you paid your money into a specific kitty. On the other end of the spectrum, welfare, food stamps, WIC etc. have no "kitty". In other words, there are hundreds of these programs that hurt society as a whole because they are not limited by a reasonable financial give and take. Plus, it eventually hurts the recipient of these funds instead of truly providing benefits. If you get a little "beer money" in your teens, twenties or thirties for life, your life is over. Your dreams, goals and appreciation for everything in life has dwindled dramatically.

Almost everything needs to be earned, at least in the first half of your life. That includes your job, house, land, recreation............ This also holds true for trust and knowledge. When certain groups are just handed a job, for instance, it is an insult to that recipient and their group. It's especially an insult to their work ethic and intelligence. Then it turns in to an insult to the entire country because every individual is part of some "group" and there will never be any synergy. It's long overdue that we should all be Americans.....period! If not the elite will continue to divide us and we will, at least, see a race war. Maybe, we should change our name to the DSA-THE DIVIDED STATES OF AMERICA.

When the ability to dream, work and achieve your goals are eliminated you destroy the soul of the people. It will be "The Emperor has no clothes" all over again. In other words all people, especially those with group protectionist status, will no longer desire to have any accountability. In fact, they will all too often try to profit from this lack of accountability! Why do you think America has more attorneys than the WHOLE WORLD PUT TOGETHER!

The top of this list of "protectionist status" will always be the super wealthy. And this list should scare the crap out of you because that list controls the following: energy, food supply and big agriculture, education, big pharmaceutical companies (who want to eliminate your ability to even buy vitamins), Wall Street, banks, finance and all other huge oligarchies that will eliminate every middle class dream. Does any of this sound familiar? It should! This is how the "Communist manifesto" describes how to divide and then conquer the people.

A little information about our "old" media. This section of real life stories may be too "heavy" for some readers so I have decided to add a little humor. This story is the only one that is NOT real and actually is a joke. Once in a while, I will read this when I give a talk about self-sufficiency and the political correctness in our media.

It goes like this: A Harley biker is riding by the zoo in Washington,

DC when he sees a little girl leaning into the lions' cage. Suddenly, the lion grabs her by the cuff of her jacket and tries to pull her inside to slaughter her under the eyes of her screaming parents. The biker jumps off his Harley, runs to the cage and hits the lion square in the nose with a powerful punch.

Whimpering from the pain the lion jumps back letting go of the girl, and the biker brings her back to her terrified parents who thank him profusely. A reporter watched the whole event. The reporter, addressing the Harley rider, says, "Sir, this was the most gallant and brave thing I've ever seen a man do in my whole life". The Harley rider replies "why, it was nothing, really, the lion was behind bars. I just saw this little kid in danger and acted as I felt right." The reporter says, "well I'll make sure this won't go unnoticed. I'm a journalist, and in tomorrow's paper I will have this story on the front page. So, what do you do for living and what political affiliation do you have?" The biker replies, "I'm a US Marine and a Republican". The journalist leaves. The following morning the biker buys the paper to see news of his actions and reads, on the front page:

U.S. MARINE ASSAULTS AFRICAN IMMIGRANT AND STEALS HIS LUNCH

That pretty much sums up the "old" media's approach to the news these days. Even if the national media puts you on T.V. they talk over you and send you chasing down some far away "rabbit hole" so you can't prove or even make your points. Their goal is to take everything you say out of context. Do you think the media, controlled by the "powers that be", use woman and minorities to disrupt, distract and prevent middle class prosperity?

What a freak show America has turned into! So why go to school? Should job interviews now be irrelevant? Will quotas and affirmative action always trump qualifications? Why get in shape for a physical job when your skills and fitness level don't even matter? Why bother with being the best at what you do if all the human resource people see is your color, sexual orientation or your gender? Why be a part of the system if there are so many aspects that are considered "no fault"? Why let a system, including the judicial system promote special rules, laws and accountability to occur based solely on victim group status? If you have no "victim group status", according to the "elite" in America, how can you possibly control your own destiny? Are we being told by "the powers that be" that we need to NOT be in the "system"? I can probably come up with at least 5,963,398 more true stories using objective facts. I do not use any subjective or emotional opinions unless I state it's my personal opinion. Besides, no one could make up these stories. These behaviors do nothing but divide America and absolutely DO NOT create equality.

Is this what Barack Obama meant by the phrase "you didn't earn it or build it". Is it so recipients of affirmative action/quotas status can feel equal?

If you look at race and gender relation indexes across the country, you will see that Obama's numbers have gotten much worse since he became president compared to today. I hear a lot of the press being concerned that he will not have a legacy. Unfortunately he will, he had the opportunity to bring America together, however he will be known as the great "divider", just as Reagan is known for being the great "communicator".

Look at job growth numbers in America. Eliminate part time and government jobs and see what we get. Incorporate, in the formula, the under employed and all the people who have dropped out of the work force and see a disaster in the making.

Who's going to want to hire anyone with victim group status when they sue or complain so much. When certain groups expect special rules, laws and accountability, there will be no barometer of achievements, no competition and no success. We will only have an overly massive sized government and oligarchies. No wonder why so many American companies are leaving America.

Chapter 4: Equality has a new definition

Let us look at a few examples of how far this facade has come regarding "equality". I am a big NFL fan so let me use an NFL analogy. Let's say one team was from Montana and let's call them the Montana "Average Joe's". Let's say they have only average skills but work well together because they try hard and practice long hours. Let's say they are all middle-class white male heterosexuals with a Christian name. Let's say they never got a job, college education, house or down payment for a home from their "daddy" or their government. Let's say they all had earned what little they had.

Now, let's call their opponents the "San Francisco Excuses" just for the fun of it. Let's say this team was made up of people from different backgrounds and all qualify for "victim group status". In other words, they had a certain skin pigmentation, sexual orientation or were female. Now let's say they got together with the referees, before the game, and said that they were given protectionist status by our government. Some called their attorneys and sued more often than the Montana Average Joe's. Some sued just when other players from around the league told a joke. Some sued because the Average Joe's got an earlier promotion or a higher paycheck even though the Average Joe's were more qualified and produced better results. I can throw in thousands of examples but, you get the point. The football game then begins...

Kickoffs are canceled. The ref says that the San Francisco Excuses gain immediate advantage because of their coveted status. The Excuses, as per the refs, only have to run 50 yards for a touchdown, while the Montana Average Joe's have to run 100 yards for a touchdown. The game continues and despite their handicap, the Average Joe's lose by only 3 points. My questions to you are:

Do you respect the San Francisco Excuses for the win?

Do you think this creates synergy with the fans, players and owners?

Do you think this makes our country better and stronger regarding work ethic and results?

Do you think, over time, the people will continue to respect the game, the players, the rules and the refs?

Do you think that any individual who plays by special rules, laws, and accountability, just because of victim group status, will be respected?

Do you think the NFL would prosper or even survive, like it has for the past several decades, if we had different rules, laws and accountability for different players and teams?

This is why the NFL is so popular. They choose the best players with the highest qualifications which puts out the best results. In this case the results are about scoring, speed, coordination, desire, determination, athletic ability and WINNING. OOPS, shouldn't have said '"winning", it's probably "politically incorrect" these days. My bad! But going back to the above questions. Of course the answer to all these questions is an obvious NO. What has been happening in our country the last 40 years is a major lowering of the standards and a rigging of the game. When you continue to lower the bar to create the illusion of equality, you bring down the quality of life for the whole country. As this phenomenon occurs, the value of everything diminishes by the day. As the "powers that be" continue to lower the bar and create division, our values get more clouded. For generations the middle-class had the majority of their equity in their homes, but over the course of the last few years, home-equity for the middle-class has been dropping like a seagull with a heart attack. The act of harmonizing the economy has ruined the middle class.

A real life example was a plan that started during the Clinton and Bush administrations when banks were forced to make loans to people who didn't qualify. This technically also allowed investors to buy houses with stated income instead of documenting their income. End result was a huge sub-prime mortgage industry that sprang up. This was the industry the globalists targeted in 2007 and 2008 for a take-down which started the real estate crash of '08 and the theft of home equity. This was mostly done in the name of diversity and equality. Apparently, their wasn't enough low income and minority home owners.

Lets look at another situation: A female Hollywood star is tired of hearing about all this "equality" and "tolerance" propaganda and she wants to do something about it because she, as a woman, is insulted. She can see that all this victim group status has and will continue to disrespect woman, minorities and any other group that shoves special treatment (rules, laws and accountability) down other people's throats. She can see, as every American, that too many people are getting jobs, keeping jobs and suing for the wrong reasons, mostly depending on their victim group status and she can notice a major lowering of standards which is dangerous to the survival of the middle class. This intelligent female can see that there will soon be a backlash so she has come out publicly and agreed to monitor a new concept that's called "real total equality". She has noticed that too many "victim/protectionist" groups have been only asking for the good, easy and convenient aspects of equality. She also notices that "tolerance" is only applicable if it goes "one way" and is stamped by the "political correct police". So, this Hollywood celebrity has announced a new program that will be implemented in this way. This woman starts to create a top 100 list of these equality behaviors. This list starts as follows:

1) All affirmative action/quotas will now be eliminated from the books. This also includes job promotions, the ability to sue and the ability to get a job based on skin color or gender or anything else other than qualifications. She feels quotas are an insult to everyone under the "protectionist/victim group" category and is even an admission of guilt by the government or anyone who refuses to these terms. She feels that it's a direct insult to their intelligence, work ethic, tenacity and principal. She notices that people are starting to not care anymore and that respect and trust are being greatly diminished. So she decides that all testing standards, mental and physical, will go back 50 years in time. She cites examples such as the "older standards" of passing a test to become a cop, firefighter, join the military and even getting into college. What sex you are, skin color or culture will no longer play a role. It will also be illegal to mention what "group" your from!

2) This woman has the guts to publicly set a new standard for hiring and firing, and creates a barometer for success that goes public. The barometer goes something like this: You will be hired for a job based on years of work experience, hard work, effort, proven results, word of honor, whether you were a quitter in any aspect of life (which shows your tenacity and loyalty), qualifications, diligence, stand for principal and competency. You'll be asked questions like, "did you pay for your own college, your land, your home, your job or business, did you pay off your school loans or was this paid for by the government or your daddy, did you get your money from a divorce/law suit or did you earn it?" Success shouldn't be measured by where you are but, where you came from compared to where you are today. "Earning it" and how you got there holds much more weight than being "put" there! This is another reason why affirmative action and quotas have been such an embarrassment to "protectionist/victim" groups.

3) Next on her list was the military. She feels that women should be in combat and have the same "action" and "mortality rates" as men. But she also feels that men and women should be separate.

They should have their own battleships, aircraft carriers, submarines, Air Force, infantry... She feels that taxpayer dollars should not pay for babies being born or killed, sexual harassment charges or any other ridiculous law suit which too often only goes to the one with the highest victim group status.

4) Next on her list was the propaganda regarding sexual activity. She is just tired of hearing how demeaning the "powers that be" have been toward women and are too often treating them like babies. She feels that since homosexual men have been able to use the argument that it's "adult, mutually, consensual sex" than it's no one's business who has sex. She feels that woman can make adult choices and have adult consequences. She argues that there are two kinds of sexual activity in this context. One is rape and the other is of course "adult, mutually, consensual sex." So, she feels that there should be the same rules, laws and accountability across the board. For example, if a wife cheats on her husband and gets impregnated, then there should not be "extra" accountability for that husband who didn't even know his wife was cheating, to pay child support when he isn't even the father. She feels this is an insult to women in general because they do the "choosing" for adult consensual sex. How the hell can there be a "sex scandal" when the sex is mutual? (If this continues to occur than the wife will pay the husband for his mistress). This Hollywood star gets some opposition from feminist organizations on this change. The feminist groups say that "it's not fair" because the man can't get pregnant. So, the Hollywood star mentions a solution. She says that since women, in general, have been such proponents of increased government regulations over the last few decades that she was going to propose a new regulation of her own. This new regulation will read: No female can have recreational sex unless the man is on an "approved" list because he has had a vasectomy. She goes a step further and suggests that all children at the age of 18 can have a voluntary vasectomy or their tubes tied and never pay taxes again or receive some other monetary encouragement. It's their choice! She would rather have voluntary population control vs. the government condoning and providing the most unethical of behaviors. (Wars, GMO foods, vaccines, chemicals, cancer, abortions, healthcare rationing...........).

5) Next on the Hollywood star's list is the equality of life expectancy. She notes that it's unfair to have women outlive men, on average, by eight years. So she announces that 100% of all medical research and nutrition advancements will now go towards increasing the average man's life expectancy. This new government program will discontinue only when men and women have true, total equality of life expectancy.

6) Next on her list is child custody and child support. From now on when a divorce occurs, 50% of the men will get total child custody and

the same goes for child support. For example, if there are 100 divorces "in a given state" for a given year (yeah right, keep dreaming) then 50% of those children go to the man, and 50% go to the women. Child support will be appropriately given using the example above. The Hollywood star agrees that there needs to be restitution paid to all of the men over the last 40 years that have been kicked out of their homes, ordered to pay the majority of the bills, and have not been able to see their children as often as the female.

7) Since it is now politically incorrect to generalize, this Hollywood star says that prisoner incarcerations must now be 50/50. You can no longer say that men commit more crimes than women....... it's sexist! So the next law on the books will state that men and women need to be incarcerated at a similar rate and do the SAME time for the same crime. Let's use the example above, "in a given state", for context. So, let's say that there are 100 crimes per year in a given state and 80 of them are done by men and 20 are done by women. This means that only 20 men can be incarcerated for their crime in that given state for that year. Isn't equality great! Now, now, now tolerance please!

8) She also mentions that poor/middle class white, heterosexual males must have as many private and public meetings, rally's and parades as every other "group".

This Hollywood star ends this list by saying "can you see how many billions of dollars the American taxpayers have wasted on this ridiculous equality propaganda. We will never be and should never want to be equal. This has only been a tool, by the elite, to divide the American people."

Of course, we could all come up with our own top 100 list, in this same context. But, for the sake of this book I need to keep each of my lists and chapters short enough to make my points and continue with all this variety. One of my objectives is to describe with real life facts and examples the economic, financial, political and social reasons for being self-sufficient. If I kept on going, I would have a book larger than "War and Peace".

So, the million dollar question here is will this celebrity be ostracized from Hollywood OR will she be revered for showing equality with honor because of her introduction to the "real total equality" program? I think we all know the answer.

Honor and Hollywood? I know it seems like a contradiction in terms but there are a few exceptions. Do you really think that Mel Gibson was ostracized from Hollywood because of a few things he said while drunk? Of course not! I think it's because he has created movies that were about honor and/or patriotism. Such as "Braveheart" and "We Were Soldiers" and "The Patriot". Even his movie "Payback" was about getting the exact amount of money that was stolen from him and not a penny more. Some other great movies about honor and patriotism are "300" and "The last Samurai". I enjoy these movies!

There are a few other movies that I also enjoy that are about individuals achieving their dreams. They were all long shots. Some examples off of the top of my head are "Invincible", "Cinderella Man" and "Rudy" mentioned earlier in the book.

I also like to discuss tenacity, inspiration and motivational perspectives and stories with others. Especially about this humble, natural, self-sufficient lifestyle. If you are interested in helping others, living off-grid, being self-sufficient and living frugally then, I have a great movie suggestion for you, "The Simple Life of Noah Dearborn". It's a about a man who is living just as I am describing above. The star of this movie is Sidney Poitier and he is a great actor. Watch it and enjoy what is truly a great simple life!

It's a shame that America has become so petty, pathetic and dumbed-down regarding political correctness. (By the way, if you ever hear a politician talking about the same "rules and laws" for everyone AND they don't mention ACCOUNTABILITY, then they are a phoney, who indirectly promotes division). Unfortunately, since equality has been shoved down everyone's throat, a list like the Hollywood star wrote above will have to be implemented in order to get equal respect for all groups. If these ideas don't happen then the word hypocrite will continue to pop up its evil head and these groups will never gain any credibility. It's analogous to some of America's elite class behaviors. How can anyone be a proponent of gun control when they hire private security firms, who carry guns to protect them? How can anyone have the audacity to use taxpayer dollars to hire security, have them carry guns, and then not allow the poor and middle class to do the same so that they can protect themselves? There is no credibility to these arguments. Are there any parents out there, who smoke cigarettes? Ever try telling your own children not to smoke? How did it go? Exactly!

I have known so many great hard-working women and minorities who are insulted by these "excuse behaviors" implemented by feminist and minority groups. I hope it satisfies these groups now knowing that their daughter can now go into battle and get raped and killed. I'm sure that every parent is now pleased with the fact that their daughters can abort their own baby in a public school setting and are especially excited that you the parent, don't even have to be notified. But don't forget that permission slip for a class trip!

I hear the despair and even regret in a lot of parents and grandparents voices today. They feel so helpless and without control that they are starting to rationalize and justify these behaviors. I often hear them say "Oh it will be okay, just different". Personally, if I were a young person today that made it into my 50s, as I am now, I would feel like I got gypped out of my life. This phoney life of electronic virtual reality is like living vicariously through another individual or should I say, machine. How will this young generation be able to feed themselves if things get tough? I don't know who to feel sorry for most, today's children or parents and grandparents having to watch all this. Live your adventures and dreams when you're young and you will have way fewer regrets in life as you get older. Nothing worthwhile is going to be easy.

What is the American dream? If the barometer for success is so smudged, what is the formula for a successful life? There are two things that the middle-class can never buy back: time and health. So, if hard work, effort, proven results, qualifications, principal, diligence and tenacity mean less every day, what's a person to do to have this "good life"? How does a person gain more free time and maintain their health?

Is the answer buying a big house in urban/suburban America? Remember, taxes, insurance and maintenance are directly proportional to the size of the house. What can we do that will not sabotage us in the end? Personally, I believe trying to live below our means while separating our needs from our wants is one way to go today. Through personal observation, I feel that at least 80% of financial success comes through discipline. (Something big government and oligarchy's don't need to have because the middle class taxpayers will bail them out.) There are obviously consequences beyond our control which include health problems, divorces (being sued), child support, death to the family breadwinner, crimes and much more. Trust me, I'm not any smarter or better or more skilled than anyone else. I'm just a regular guy. My SAT scores were probably the lowest in the country. In fact, I was pretty much only a "C" student. OK, I'll admit I played a lot, especially during the autumn months! But, I still attended and graduated from three colleges, and enjoyed a relatively successful career. I had a plan of action and worked through my personal struggles and challenges. And, most of all, I tried to live below my means. This is not what the kids are being taught today, nor have been taught for some time.

The beneficiaries and defenders of the status quo/protectionist status are doing just the opposite. They are also insulting the work ethic, principal, and intelligence of people who do not have the luxury of protectionist status or victim status. They claim they are seeking a colorblind society and yet they secure the continuance of a biased race and gender classification through this status. I think each of us could write a book on the hypocrisies by the defenders of the status quo.

It shouldn't matter what your race, gender or anything else is. If you give your word of honor, vow or oath everyone should have the same rules, laws and accountability.

Why is it that the politicians who claim to fight for the poor and middle class always distance themselves from those people when socializing. Why do they hang out with the super wealthy? How can you say you're fighting for the poor when you charge $30,000 per plate for a campaign event?

How can anyone say that the government discriminates against black America when we have elected a black president two times and we have a black attorney general. Not to mention the fact that the percentage of black federal workers far outnumbers the percentage of black population here in America.

How may times have you seen proponents of big government and higher taxes not practice what they preach? Do you remember Tim Geitner (head of the Treasury Department) and Charles Wrangle (once ran the Ways and Means committee) ? Do you remember they both got caught being tax cheats? Do you know that congress exempts itself from Obama Care?

How can the "powers that be" tell the world that it is a privilege to be an American when the word "illegal" is so ambiguous? Millions of people have paid tens of thousands of dollars to wait in their home country and hope for communication to enter our country legally. At the same time, these people, who are paying for the privilege to become citizens are watching America debate over allowing people who sneak into our country illegally to become citizens.

Why is it that in America you need a drivers license/ID to buy alcohol and cash a check but, you don't need a drivers license/ID to vote?

The hypocrisies filed under the headline of political correctness are endless today. It is up to you the American people to draw a line in the sand and say "no more". We shouldn't waste another penny of taxpayer dollars on any more debates or discussions until the truth is told.

Civil right's policies were designed to ensure that Americans should be judged on the basis of individual merit, but are now too often dividing people by race and gender............and too many people are falling for this divisive trick. Civil rights are inherently individual rights defined as a right to life, liberty, and the pursuit of happiness. These rights are held equally under law. But if we have separate laws not just for people who have "victim group status" but also the super wealthy, that leaves a particular group subject to discrimination, and that group is the poor and middle class white male, heterosexual, who have Christian names. This is the only "non-protectionist" group.

We are now left with lots of division and very little synergy. Amendments to the Constitution and the Bill of Rights guarantee that "No state shall make or enforce any law which shall abridge the privileges or immunities of citizens of the United States; nor shall any state deprive any person of life, liberty, or property, without due process of law; nor deny any person within its jurisdiction the equal protection of the laws." But when groups of people are given special privilege through corporate structure and government entitlement, life, liberty, property, and even due process are being erased for many of us.

By the way, Judge Andrew Napalitano or Stewart Rhodes (founder of Oath keepers) would make a great Attorney General for America because they really know our Constitution.

I have spoken to a lot of corporate presidents and V.P's from numerous industries over the years during my travels. I have asked them why they are moving their companies out of America and their answers might surprise you. The national media tells us it's all about cheap labor, but according to these businessmen, the issues of political correctness trump that. They have told me, many times, that there are too many regulations, lawsuits, and corruption from big corporate oligarchies and government and outsourcing simply erases most of those problems. It may still sound mercenary, but think about it; we have created so much red tape and bureaucracy in America that most industries can barely function here! Not to mention that we now have the highest corporate tax rates in the world. Plus, American attorneys have turned "liability paranoia" into a gigantic business.

It's obvious that this is also part of the plan. It would be so simple to penalize companies for leaving the U.S. but they get too many monetary benefits from leaving and too many palms in Washington are getting greased! The "powers that be" are trying to collapse America through over regulation and corruption and it's up to us to create synergy and save our culture.

Let's use Martha Stewart as a quick example. She started baking pastries out of her home to begin her fame and fortune. Since 6,487,739 new regulations, if you started a food business out of your home today you would be making license plates instead of baking cakes (unless you're supplying them with a hidden file).

To reiterate, when a country lowers its bar of standards and expectations, the quality of life descends for all but the top 2% of the super wealthy. In fact, they buy up everything for pennies on the dollar after everyone goes into foreclosure. When you have a country with more attorneys than the whole world combined, a corrupt and paid-off judicial system, a corrupt oligarchy which rotates big corporate CEOs and high government officials like revolving doors, there can be little middle-class success, prosperity, or quality of life.

With inflation about to go through the roof, increased national debt, not enough good jobs to go around, credit limits going down, interest rates soon to rise, food prices increasing, taxes increasing, high energy costs, less drinkable uncontaminated water available, compromised GDP to debt ratio and a devaluation of our currency what will be your plan of action? We are all going to have to make sacrifices if we want to achieve our goals or even survive. The middle-class is on the brink of extinction and it's up to you to live below your means, learn to produce, save, or become extinct along with those who have no plan. By the way, we actually have stagflation now. Which is the worst of deflation and inflation. We will still have less disposable income in the long run.

How about our elected and even non-elected government officials? Wow, do we have "electile" dysfunction in America or what? If you've got big bucks or big money backing you, go ahead and run for office.

Isn't it all about equality and being "liked"? It's amazing to me that one of the most important criteria for these phoney election polls is "likability". How frigging ridiculous have we become? So if Mr. Smith were running for office and had on an expensive suit, had lots of money, shook everybody's hands, told you how attractive and smart you were and told every group what they wanted to hear, does that mean he could get elected because of "likability"? Maybe I should buy a "left-handed smoke shifter" so I can blow smoke up everyone's ass. How far have we fallen? When a propaganda word such as "likability" trumps attributes like hard work, proven results, experience, word of honor, qualifications, tenacity and principal............................ it's over! When truths are banned because it may hurt someone's feelings who has "victim group status".........it's over!

Maybe the middle class should conduct a "poll" of their own. The question should read: How much money would the average American need to retire comfortably? If the answer is $3 million then "the people" should remove all that extra net worth from the "powers that be" and return it to the middle class from whom it was taken. Equality baby!

Maybe the "people" should require that all laws be "non-exempt". If the "powers that be" pass a health care law they need to be subject to it too. Pay into Social Security and have to use it, no more "special pensions".....

Just think about this. What if you are a poor/middle class white male, heterosexual with a Christian name. Lets say you never inherited anything, never hired anyone, never fired anyone, was never in management.............Do you deserve to be so discriminated against because of what some rich white guys did generations ago, especially ones that you aren't even related to? I wonder who the "powers that be" are going to attack in 30 years? Maybe the children of today's wealthy? Doubt it! Political Correctness has destroyed America!

It's obvious that most people do not track forex markets, precious metals or debt to GDP ratio, or true unemployment, all of which expose the trappings of the globalist ideology.

The great frustration I see is the fact that many "low information" voters are rarely on the same page (or even the same book) during political and economic discussions. When we see the nature of the false left/right paradigm, they see "free democracy". When we see a tidal wave of destructive debt, they see a responsible government printing and spending in order to protect our best interests. Where we see totalitarianism or fascism, they see "safety". Where we see dollar devaluation, they see dollar strength and longevity. Ultimately, because the average unaware citizen is stricken by the disease of normalcy bias and living within the doldrums of a statistical fantasy world, they simply have no point of reference by which to grasp the truth when exposed to it. It's like trying to explain the concept of 'color' to a man who has been blind since birth.

Americans in particular are prone to reactionary dismissal when exposed to facts that disrupt their misconceptions. Our culture has experienced a particularly prosperous age, not necessarily free from all trouble, but generally spared from widespread mass tragedy for a generous length of time. This tends to breed within societies an overt and unreasonable expectation of ease. It generates apathy and laziness, and a crushing blubberous slothful zombieism subservient to the establishment and the status quo. Even the most striking of truths struggle to penetrate this smoky force field of duplicitous funk.

There are very immediate dangers in several potential economic events that are likely to take place in the near future, including the exit of peripheral countries from the European Union, the conflict between austerity and socialist spending in France and Germany, the developing bilateral trade agreements between China and numerous other countries which cut out their reliance on the U.S. dollar, and the likelihood that the Federal Reserve announcement of (Infinite QE) will create a rush of new fiat currency into our system. All of these elements are leading in one very particular direction: the end of the Greenback as the world reserve currency.

When making this assertion, some people (many of them indignant) question how it would be even remotely possible that the dollar could be replaced at all. The concept is so outside their narrow world view that many cannot fathom it.

To be sure, the question is a viable one. How could the dollar be unseated? That said, a few hours of light research would easily produce the answer, but this tends to be too much work for the fly-by-night financial skeptic.

The Dollar A Safe Haven?

This ongoing lunacy is based on multiple biases. For some, the dollar represents America, and a collapse of our currency would suggest a failure of the republic, and thus, a failure by them as individual Americans who live vicariously through the exploits of their government. By extension, it becomes patriotic to defend the dollar's honor and deny any information that might suggest it is on a downward spiral.

Others see how the investment world clings to the dollar as a kind of panic room; a protected place where one's saving will be insulated from crisis. However, just because a majority of day trading investors are gullible enough to overlook the Greenback's pitfalls does not mean those dangerous weaknesses disappear.

There is only one factor that shields the dollar from implosion, and that is its position as the world reserve currency. (All world currencies must be converted to the U.S. Dollar at current market values before they can make purchases of oil on the world markets.) Without this exalted status, the currency's value vanishes. Backed by nothing but massive and unpayable debt, it sits frighteningly idle, like a time bomb, waiting for the moment of ignition.

The horrifying nature of the dollar is that it is only valuable so long as foreign investors believe that we will pay back the considerable debts that we (the American taxpayer at the behest of our criminally run Treasury) owe, and that we will not hyper-inflate in the process. If they EVER begin to see their purchases of dollars and treasuries as a gamble instead of an investment, the facade falls away. Yet, again this year, Congress and the Executive Branch are at odds over the expansion of the debt ceiling, which has been raised to levels beyond the 100% of GDP mark.

Barack Obama has made claims that increases in the debt ceiling are normal and that most presidents are prone to hiking the barrier every once in a while. Yet, back in 2006, when George W. Bush increased debt limits, Obama had this to say:

"The fact that we are here today to debate raising America's debt limit is a sign of leadership failure. It is a sign that the U.S. Government can't pay its own bills... Instead of reducing the deficit, as some people claimed, the fiscal policies of this administration and its allies in Congress will add more than $600 million in debt for each of the next five years... Increasing America's debt weakens us domestically and internationally. Leadership means that 'the buck stops here.' Instead, Washington is shifting the burden of bad choices today onto the backs of our children and grandchildren. America has a debt problem and a failure of leadership. Americans deserve better."

For once, Barack and I agree on something. Too bad the man changes his rhetoric whenever it's to his advantage.....as too many politicians do.

Today, Obama now asserts that raising the debt ceiling is not an opening for more government spending, but an allowance for the government to pay bills it has already accrued. This is disingenuous and hypocritical prattle. Obama is well aware as are many in Congress, that as long as the Federal Government is able to raise the debt ceiling whenever it suits them, they can increase spending with wild abandon. It's like handing someone a credit card with no maximum limit. For most men, the temptation would be irresistible. Therefore, one can predict with 100% certainty that U.S. spending will never truly be reduced, and that our national debt will mount in tandem until we self destruct.

How has this trend been able to continue for so long? The private central bank, known as the Federal Reserve, has created the fiat machine by which all economic depravity is possible. Currently, the Federal Reserve is the number one holder of U.S. debt; It creates its own capital. It prints its wealth from thin air. The dollar, thus, has become its own lynchpin. The secretive institution, which has never been subject to a full audit, is now monetizing endless debt mechanisms with paper promises. What value would any intelligent investor put on such a fraudulent economic system? How can "Main Street" afford to take any more risks with anything "on paper"? This is especially true for the stock market. The big money and big connections always know when to pull out of the stock market, but Main Street doesn't get this inside information until it's too late.

The epic dysfunction of the dollar is rooted in its reliance on perception rather than tangible wealth or strong fundamentals. It is, indeed, like any other fiat unit, with all the inevitable pitfalls built into its structure. This fall began when tangible gold no longer backed the dollar. Ironically, the value of the Dollar Index is measured not by its intrinsic buying power, or its historical buying power, but its arbitrary buying power in comparison with other collapsing fiat currencies.

The argument I hear most often when pointing out the calamitous path of the dollar is that it is the go-to safe haven in response to the crisis in Europe. What the financially inept don't seem to grasp is that the shifting of savings back and forth between the Euro and the Dollar is just as irrelevant to our currency's survival as it is to Europe's. BOTH currencies are in decline, and this is evident by the growing inflationary pressures on both sides of the Atlantic. Ask any consumer in Greece, Spain, France, or the UK how shelf prices have changed in the past four years, and they will say the exact same thing as any consumer in the U.S.; costs have gone way up. Therefore, it makes sense to compare the Dollar's value not to the Euro, or to the Yen, but something more practical, like the dollar of the past.

In 1972, just as Nixon was removing the dollar from the last vestiges of the gold standard, a new car cost an average of $4500. A home cost around $40,000. A gallon of gas was .36 cents. A loaf of bread was .25 cents. A visit to the doctor's office was $25. Wages were certainly lower, but a dollar bought considerably more than it does today. Now, the gap between wages and inflation is insurmountable. The average family is unable to keep up with the flash flood of rising prices.

Every time the elite wants to maintain their power (status quo) they literally sell tons of worthless paper gold and silver to keep the physical prices down. There is an obvious manipulation and epidemic of naked shorts. Very soon the Comex will be considered illegitimate and physical gold/silver prices will sky-rocket. There is a very big movement towards tangibility in this country because there is so little trust in the "powers that be".

According to the historic buying power of the Dollar, the currency is a poor safe-haven investment. With the advent of bailouts and debt monetization through quantitative easing, its devaluation has been expedited dramatically. The Fed has left the door open for a final destructive round of publicly announced QE, soon weakening the Dollar to near death.

The question then arises: why do foreign countries continue to buy in on the greenback?

The Dollar Dump Has Already Begun

One of my favorite arguments by those defending the Dollar is the assertion that no foreign country would dare to dump the currency because they are all too dependent on U.S. trade. To answer the question above, the reality is that foreign countries ARE already calmly and quietly dumping the Dollar as a global trade instrument. China, in tandem with other BRICS nations, has been covertly removing the greenback as the primary trade unit through bilateral deals since 2010. First with Russia, and now with the whole of the ASEAN trading bloc and numerous other markets, including Japan. China in particular has been preparing for this eventuality since 2005, when they introduced the first Yuan denominated bonds. The bonds were considered a strange novelty back then, especially because China had so much surplus savings that it seemed outlandish for them to take on treasury debt. Today, the move makes a whole lot more sense. China and the BRICS nations today openly call for a worldwide shift away from the Dollar.

With the global proliferation of the Yuan, and the conversion of the Chinese economy from dependence on exports (especially to the West) towards a more consumer based system, the Chinese have effectively decoupled from their reliance on U.S. markets. Would a collapse in the U.S. hurt China's economy? Yes. Would they still survive? Oh yes.

Central banks around the world, especially China, are buying gold and silver like it's going to be extinct in 3 years......maybe it will. It's plain to see that the worlds' central banks don't trust each other and so this is why they are getting their gold back from other countries. It will be interesting to watch the maneuvering since so much of this gold has been leased multiple times over to different owners. As these currency wars continue (central banks printing too much money and devaluing their currencies), more of the other central banks are going to buy gold.

To be clear, the true threat to the Dollar's supremacy is due not only to the constant printing by the private Federal Reserve (though that is a nightmare in the making), but the loss of faith in our currency as a whole. The Fed does not need to throw Dollars from helicopters to annihilate our currency; all they have to do is create doubt in its viability.

The bottom line? A Dollar collapse is not theory but undeniable fact in motion at this moment, driven by concrete actions on the part of the very nations that have until recently propped up our debt obligations. It is only a matter of time before the Dollar diminishes and fades away. In fact, every fiat currency in the world has a limited life span. All signs point to a loss of reserve status in the near term.

What Will Replace The Dollar?

My next favorite argument in defense of the Greenback is the assertion that there is "no currency in a position to take the Dollar's place if it falls."

First of all, this is based on a very naïve assumption that the Dollar will not fall unless there is another currency to replace it. I'm not sure who made that rule up, but the Dollar is perfectly capable of being flushed without a replacement in the wings. Economic collapse does not follow logical guidelines or the personal pet peeves of random man-child economists.

There is, most likely, already a convenient replacement ready to roll forward. The IMF has for a couple of years now openly called for the retirement of the dollar as the world reserve currency, to be supplanted by the elitist organization's very own "Special Drawing Rights" (SDR's).

The SDR is a paper mechanism created in the early 1970's to replace gold as the primary means of international trade between foreign governments. Today, it has morphed into a basket of currencies which is recognized by almost every country in the world and is in a prime position to take the Dollar's place in the event that the Dollar loses reserve status. The SDR today could also be backed by some gold, oil or other tangible resources. They may even try to roll out a new treasury note to replace the Federal Reserve note, the bottom line is the shelf life of the Dollar looks short.

The only thing I can see saving our present definition of the dollar is a small miracle. It would have to be a massive re-evaluation, to the upside, of another fiat currency that the U.S. owns a lot of. An example would be the Iraqi Dinar. If this currency gets re-valued positively and is put toward Americas debt, then maybe the U.S. Dollar could be saved.

So, now that we think a replacement for the Dollar is ready to go, the next obvious question is - Why would global elites destroy a useful monetary tool like the Dollar? Why kill the goose that "lays the golden eggs"?

People who ask this question are simply unable to see outside the fiscal box they have been placed in. For global bankers, a paper currency is not important. It is expendable. Like a layer of snake skin; as the snake grows, it sheds the old and dons the new.

The bottom line is, men who promote the philosophy of globalization greatly desire the exaltation of a global currency. The Dollar, though a creation of a central bank, is still a semi-sovereign monetary unit. It is an element that is getting in the way of the application of the global currency dynamic. I find it rather convenient (at least for those who subscribe to globalism) that the Dollar is now in the midst of a perfect storm of decline just as the IMF is ready to introduce it's latest implementation of a fiat concoction in the form of the SDR. I find the blind faith in the

Dollar's lifespan to be rife with delusion. It is not a matter of opinion or desire, but a matter of fact that currencies in such tenuous positions fall, and are in the end replaced. I believe that the evidence shows that this is not random chance, but a deliberate process leading towards the globalist ideal; total centralization of the world under an unaccountable governing body which operates a global monetary system utterly devoid of transparency and responsibility. The bottom line is the middle class will lose ground during any transition.

The Dollar was a median step towards a newer and more corrupt ideal. Its time is nearly over. This information is out in the open, it is admitted, and it is being activated upon as you read this. The speed at which this disaster occurs is really dependent on the speed at which our government, along with our central bank, decides to expedite doubt. Doubt in a currency is a dire omen, costing not just investors, but an entire society. America is at the very edge of such a moment. The naysayers can scratch and bark all they like, but the financial life of a country serves no person's emphatic hope. It burns like a fire. Left unwatched and unchecked, it grows uncontrollable and wild, until finally, there is nothing left to fuel its hunger, and it finally chokes in a haze of confusion and dread…

How long do you think we have before the Dollar is gone? By 2020, the US Government will be spending more annually on debt interest than the total combined military budgets of China, Britain, France, Russia, Japan, Germany, Saudi Arabia, India, Italy, S. Korea, Brazil, Canada, Australia, Spain, Turkey and Israel. Do you think it will last that long?

Does the term "Ponzi scheme" come to mind? Just asking. Is it just a coincidence that our Federal Government has created a document like the NDAA? (The National Defense Authorization Act). Laws that allow ordinary American citizens to be taken from their homes and put in jail with no jury or trial……..and even be executed? When governments print and spend money, it just turns into currency. This robs the middle class of time, health, liberty and freedom which are the real and accurate barometers of true wealth. No interest in our pockets plus inflation on the shelves is a recipe for the perfect storm.

A quick note on the stock market and economic health. Do you think the stock market is standing on it's own merit or do you think there is artificial manipulation based on the "printing" of money? If this is real than why is the VIX index going up this spring. This is the volatility index which usually moves down when the stock market goes up. Plus, the BDI (the Baltic Dry Index) is going down. This index reflects the cost of shipping dry goods overseas. If the stock market and economy is growing then their should be an increased demand for shipping goods.

Here are the perfect "four winds" of the storm/bubble....which will implode first? The stock market, bond market, our Dollar or our loss as the Dollar's worlds reserve currency?

Chapter 6: The importance of helping others

It seems obvious to me (and hopefully to most people out there) that the "powers that be" are doing everything imaginable to divide and conquer America. That is to say that they are deliberately attempting to obliterate everything that made our country successful at its inception. Our culture, traditions, heritage, American definitions of common words, the middle class; all of it is on the chopping block. It is clear this process of degradation has created a legitimate lack of community in America. So, the first thing that came to my mind was to write a book that would make people "think" independently versus blindly "follow" the mainstream, so that they might break free from establishment conditioning. I believe that every individual has strengths, skills and talents that are unique. I also believe that there shouldn't be one individual or a super wealthy oligarchy making the rules for everyone else. (Most of these high and mighty elite don't even practice what they preach). If we as a society could think outside the box, we could truly have diversity instead of this "cookie-cutter/follower/politically correct" mentality that is so prevalent today.

What if all 50 states ran their operations differently? Not everyone is the same so let's help more people around the country by giving them options on where to live and how to live. Over time we could assess the pros and cons to see which states were the most successful based on trial and error. Often there is no "right" answer except "it depends"; so, let's get more people chiming in on economy, finances, politics and social ideas instead of creating a dictatorship which governs only the poor and middle class. More people would be able to share ideas and different states could specialize or discover a better way of life, a life where more of the people could control their own destiny.

I had discussions with a few people about writing a book that would give what's left of the middle class an option for better living, especially people who already have an affinity for nature. Some of them suggested I write a book on off grid living. My off-grid talks in the past have inspired people to move from the metropolitan areas like New York City to other rural parts of the country. It would seem that many people are interested in the off-grid lifestyle or a life that is just simpler.

This economy has wiped out too many people's homes, equity, retirement, savings and dreams. What's left of the middle class is looking for some kind of alternative to the faulty "American Dream" (and if they're not, they should be). Last year alone we had about 250 visitors to my off-grid farm; some of them friends and acquaintances, and many travelers searching for a better future. They either read an article about my lifestyle or heard a talk I've done. I've been asked why I show people how to undertake this particular lifestyle with things getting so bad in our country today. I believe that if we all dig out caves to live in and forget our fellow man, then everything good about America will die. Don't be afraid to be on some "list" when you have honorable dreams of helping someone. (I can guarantee you that we are all on some list anyway!) You're better off taking a stand for principle than to die, slowly laying on your couch watching the "blue light" and hoping nobody sees you. We are approaching a kind of "zombie phenomenon" very quickly. I often share the very tangible benefits-both from a fiscal and health perspective-that independence and living off the grid provide. This is one way to ensure that other people understand that they have a choice outside of the crumbling mainstream.

For example, growing your own produce is a fantastic, life-improving activity that many people simply do not undertake. It has been on my list as an interest and hobby for quite some time but there are other benefits to it beyond recreation. Gardening alone kills several birds with a single stone. We save money on produce. We eat healthy, non-GMO foods with no pesticides and no chemicals. (If you have children how can you even make an argument?) I probably spend only 30 to 40 min. per day gardening and yet I still reap the health benefits of moving around. I get the satisfaction of honing important survival skills. Last but not least, I can't really put into words how satisfying it is to pick a tomato, squash, cucumber, asparagus or cabbage and eat it raw right from the garden. Eating raw vegetables is where the majority of the vitamins, minerals, enzymes and health benefits reside. If you have gardening skills, share your knowledge, trade heirloom seeds, and spread the wealth. This skill is the best way to help Americans with nutrition.

I get a lot of satisfaction from showing other folks how to live off the land. This lifestyle is quite varied and includes everything from teaching people raised bed gardening, building inexpensive greenhouses, composting, alternative energy, animal husbandry, hunting and fishing, skinning and butchering, to cultivation of edible and medicinal plants.... Many Americans are beginning to feel the financial crunch and independent-living knowledge could indeed help them to reverse the course of their lives. Unfortunately, too many people have reached the "giving up point" and don't want to be helped, for reasons that are difficult to comprehend.

I occasionally use the analogy of the sinking of the Titanic in my lectures on self-sufficient/off grid living. Do you remember the Titanic? Of course! In any crisis there are three types of people. Say these three types are lounging on the Titanic and they receive the news that the ship is "going down". The first type of person reacts with basic shock. His jaw drops, he is unable to speak, and he pisses his pants. The second type of person is in total denial. He was taught that catastrophic events only happen to "other people"- others on the opposite side of the world. He responds with cynicism and attacks the messenger as a crazed Chicken Little, "conspiracy theorist". He was taught that it's not politically correct to believe in or give credence to such warnings, and so he walks off in a huff and goes back to the ship's bar to get drunk. (He is often the type who gets 99% of his information from the "mainstream media"). Then, there is the third type of person. This is the type of person that I'm trying to reach with this book. This person hears about the ship going down and starts ripping apart furniture and walls to build a raft. Even if his probability of survival is less than 1%, this type of person will never give up. If you are this type of person you know that you could never quit. You will never give up on survival or on your dream.

I spend a lot of time giving financial counsel and sharing strategies with people on living below their means: that is to say, knowing the fine lines between needs and wants. I talk about a lot of issues but concentrate on the financial aspects that are unique to the individual I'm counseling.

I often discuss amortization schedules, meaning an itemized breakdown of a loan or mortgage. It's amazing how many people don't know that the first 7 ½ years on a 30 year mortgage is about 98% interest. I try to invest time with people so they can invest wisely in their homes and put money into principal immediately. I personally scrutinized my own amortization schedule for hours. This gave me the opportunity to know where and how much money to put into principal. Because of this, I was able to pay off my first home in two and half years. I've been out of debt since.

I also share ideas on retirement. When George Bush passed a law that you could buy land with pretax money, I was one of the first people in the country to do it. Because of that timing, I was able to dodge the stock market crash of 2008. There are some restrictive regulations, of course, the most important being that you can't live on a parcel of land you buy with your IRA/401(k). However, you can buy an adjacent piece of land to live on and expand your privacy while closely monitoring your investment.

In general people have no faith or trust in the stock market or paper investments today, which is why concrete land investments are so important. It's part of the tangibility concept I talk about often. I have been helping people with their finances since my late 20's and am proud to say I have never charged anybody one penny. People call me out of the blue for advice, and I am glad to give it when I can.

The process of helping others is sometimes difficult. I love the outdoors, and am often entranced by the outdoor life. In other words, I'm so happy and excited to be out in the forest that I've always had issues with giving other important people in my life enough of my time. A little humor here........... I have a plaque on my cabin that reads "give a man a fish and you'll feed him for a day, show a man how to fish and you will never see him again". Yep, I love to hunt and fish! I remember coming home from work so many times and practically tearing off my suit and tie so I could put on my camouflage, grab my bow and arrow and run up the mountain behind my house. So the message here is, if you're like me and have a significant other, you need to inform them of your passion for the outdoors and the off-grid life very early on. (IF that's what you choose to do). You need to make it clear that they have to be one of two types of people. They need to be either extremely tolerant of your need to be in the outdoors or they need to have the same passion and enthusiasm for the outdoors as you.

I have to say that I've been extremely lucky over the last 12 years because I have met a woman who is almost as passionate about the outdoors as myself. You can't help somebody and you cannot live with somebody, if they think they can "change you" over time. There's something about nature that is in the heart and soul. Most people who live in very rural areas love everything that is natural and can't get enough of it.

It is also important to try and give back, especially if you're older. Unfortunately, America has lost the mentor/protege relationship. In Eastern countries, experience, knowledge, and advice is revered and welcomed. In America, if you are older "the powers that be" say you shouldn't be alive. (Wait until Obama Care kicks in, you will see life expectancy drop like a rock.) The only exception to this rule is if you are very wealthy. Personally, I think you should give back even if you're not wealthy. If you have advice, certain skills, talents or just have a dream of having a low impact lifestyle with nature, you should help others. Sadly, like in my Titanic analogy, two thirds of the people out there are very difficult to help.

I notice in today's youth, specifically in a lot of generation X and Y, an expectation of instant gratification. For example, when these young people see my garden they are awed by its beauty but, as they walk away they are often saying "wow, that's a lot of work!" I also notice that when young people get hold of some cash, whether they earned it or it was given to them, the first thing they do is go out and blow it on themselves. They just spend it on something stupid, non-tangible and irrelevant. Instead of saving it for a rainy day, or maybe investing it like I did to establish their first bit of equity. (I bought a trailer in a trailer park at around 22 years old........it wasn't much but I had equity). Or maybe saying "thank you" to their parents for raising them. I also felt it was necessary to pay for my own college.

I graduated from three separate colleges, paying my own way by working and taking out school loans and all loans have been paid off many years ago. By the age of 32, I was 100% out of debt. Stories like these are the best way to help young people. It teaches them about time leverage for investments and the great reward of helping others. (Time leverage benefits are assuming that their aren't any "bubbles" in that market and that prices are going up and not down.)

I want to make it perfectly clear that I'm just an average guy. I don't consider myself having any special skills and talents. The difference between myself and some others is that I know what I've done, I'm aware of where I came from, and I know what kind of life I want to live. Whether I'm meeting someone on the street, am a guest on radio show, or giving a lecture on self-sufficiency, I am always trying to help people with advice for going after their dream. I want to urge everyone in this time of turmoil to try to give back and help people. Even if you think you have no advice to give, you do, so go out there and surprise yourself. Having a college degree means nothing now days, I would rather learn from people who are self-sufficient rather than from people who have huge houses and the debt to go with them. That's why I respect most Montanans, they can do anything.

I see the despair and uncertainty in people's eyes and hear it in their voices. It's plain to anyone that the middle class is losing every bit of ground they have worked so hard to gain. I'm hoping that this book can motivate and inspire some while giving others ideas on a new rural lifestyle.

I feel so blessed, despite my health, to have the opportunity to live the way I have always envisioned living since I was a teenager. I don't know how long my body will hold up but I will not give up easily. I hope some of you reading this will decide to go for your dream, even if it is as humble as mine. I hope some of you, even with compromised health, can get some motivation to leave your couch and the "blue light". (Personally, the "blue light" phenomenon should be used more for the older folks past 55, the younger people should be outside playing sports, hunting, fishing and camping). Can you believe there are commercials on T.V. practically begging young people to go out and "play for 60 minutes per day". Wow, that's a mind blower! When I was young I played for 18 hours per day and still couldn't get enough. The young of today will have so many regrets when they get to my age, it's sad ! I hope that some of you will revisit nature and its renewable resources. It's a lifestyle that can make you healthier in mind and body. I hope that Americans will eventually leave behind the crutch of pharmaceuticals and live free in nature.

The recent Connecticut shootings that killed 29 people, including so many little children, was a tragedy facilitated by the horrors of psychotropic drugs. In fact, most mass shooting tragedies occur because of anti-psychotic drugs. When people are on these drugs their minds can be altered too easily. Even when I was a pharmaceutical representative, I was always preaching against these drugs. Too many people are killing others and themselves when under their influence. Please don't take these mind altering drugs. The best way to help these people is to introduce them to nature, teach them what you know, be a mentor. If you have the influence to motivate these people to get off of these terrible drugs, you can truly change their lives. Try changing your living habits, instead of the chemical workings of your brain and see how that works out instead. Try moving out to the country, living below your means and enjoying what nature has to offer. I can't tell you how much fun I have everyday with my self sufficient lifestyle. Every day in nature is different. Everyday I walk down to the river that runs through my property and it's always different. Different water flow, clarity, wildlife-this lifestyle is truly an adventure in variety.

I have also been fortunate to harvest many big game animals. I won't say much about this until I get to the "hunting/fishing adventure" chapter. But, I do need to mention that I have given away at least 50% of the wild game meat that I have harvested over the years. I have to say that everyone who has received wild game from me has been very appreciative. It makes me feel good to help people.

There are many who advocate the "green" lifestyle for others but not themselves and have many vehicles, planes (even jets), huge houses, but admonish us for our energy consumption! They preach global warming, which has little to do with greenhouse gases, and want you to live their "ideal" of the perfect society. They present themselves as a helping hand, but in reality, they want to dictate your future. They want power, not peace!

A word to the wise: If someone gives you advice that they don't follow, or preaches a lifestyle that they don't practice, ignore them and then tell them to shove it! The establishment is already filled with too many hypocrites. We use 200 gallons of water every 8 to 12 days in my cabin; can Al Gore say that or any of the other "greenies" ? These hypocrites don't even live off grid and wouldn't ever dream of making these sacrifices themselves.

You will see that so many people in our country have an agenda and most of it is about money, control and power. It doesn't matter if their agendas will destroy America's culture, traditions or heritages. It doesn't matter if these agendas will even kill millions and millions of Americans. It seems that political correctness can be defined by many things: It could be the elimination of family and God from the American people....; It could be the "powers that be" want to reduce American and human population....; It could be any lobbying, legislation or corrupt force which funnels money away from the middle class to the super wealthy or government. It could mean a lot more and no matter how you slice it, it will mean death for America's middle class.

Just remember that no one owes us another day. So, if you are one of the lucky ones who has achieved your dreams and goals, spend some time each day trying to help others. Communities and churches should be putting up "barter boards" to help people in need and also saving up food storage for rough times. There is a lot of concern regarding the future of commerce in this country. Get together with people and discuss tools for commerce in case the worst happens. If a collapse of any sort happens, we need to have plans for "money" and "synergy". Look at this situation not as the end of time, but a possible liberation for the middle class.

My overall point is, it's pretty obvious that we are a divided country and we need to get back to synergy. We all need to spend time helping our fellow man but we have to do it in a way that benefits society now and into the future, rather than just for the moment.

Let me start by asking middle-class America a question: are you better off today than you thought you would be?

Did you believe that your home equity would be higher? Did you think your IRA/401(k) would be higher? How about your savings and investment portfolio? Did you have trust in your employer, your brokerage firm, your hedge fund, your government? Are you succeeding as fast as you hoped you would? What are your financial prospects for the age of 30, 40, 50, 60? Are you out of debt? Did you get out of debt early in life in order to take advantage of time leverage on your assets? Are you in control of your own destiny?

If the answer to any of these questions is disappointing, maybe you should look at a different game plan altogether, instead of clinging to false ideals of some fabricated version of the "American Dream".

Have you ever thought about taking steps to become more self-sufficient or to get healthier? How about a lifestyle that dovetails your recreation with your own survival, from planting and harvesting, to hunting and fishing, to energy independence, to all around self reliance? This philosophy probably sounds utterly alien to many Americans in our modern era of apathetic convenience and immediate gratification. However, the time has come for us to accept that we as a culture have been lied to. We were force fed a world view that never truly was. We were told that if we worked within the guidelines of the system, played by the rules, and followed the instructions promoted by the mainstream, then we would be safe and happy. Today, in the midst of an expanding economic crisis, too many people are neither....

After a person comes to understand this reality and accepts it as undeniable fact, an obvious question arises: what do we do now?

The first answer to this quandary is to acquire that which we have been fooled into avoiding for decades: rural property. First of all, 90% of all Americans live in urban/suburban areas. Only 10% live in rural areas. Can you imagine how ugly it would be when we have an economic collapse? Remember the Great Depression? 80% lived rural, only 20% urban at that time. Of the millions that subsist within an urban environment, few, if any, are even remotely self sufficient. As our nation deteriorates fiscally, it may be prudent to consider whether you want to be trapped amongst the hungry and angry hordes, or amongst the predominantly better fed and better equipped in rural locations.

For those who see Off Grid and Homestead Farming as an outlandish lifestyle, I would suggest they look around themselves for a moment; this is certainly not a safe economic time to be a follower. Just think of the benefits to our country if more people would become self-sufficient and healthier by removing themselves from the grid, from the cities, and from the corrupt establishment system.

What kind of land should you purchase?

Look for land with a lot of character! In other words, land with lots of variety. The three most important features regarding the land I chose in Northwest Montana were water, low elevation, and semi-close to a very small town. I live only 4 miles from a small town with super markets, county services, doctors and much more.

Having an abundant water source nearby is priority number one. Not only do I have a quality well, but I also have a small river running through my property. I simply can't fathom why some folks, who are otherwise very intelligent people, choose arid locations with little water availability as the location for their homesteads. By doing so, they have already tipped the odds against themselves.

With a river in close proximity, I can harvest some water with a bucket, or harvest some fish with a line and reel. If you have the opportunity and the financial ability, always snap up land near a natural water source.

Well water is the next best thing to a lake or river. I found early in my research, when scouring Montana, that certain areas have aquifers that were second to none. The ease of digging a well is usually dependent upon elevation. The higher the elevation, the more trouble you are going to run into, and the more expensive the process will end up being. My cabin sits at about 2700 feet above sea level and the small-town I talked of earlier is about 2600 feet. All of the larger towns/cities in Montana are much higher in elevation. Missoula is the lowest elevation of the Montana "cities" at approximately 3200 feet. The benefits in living at a lower elevation are obvious when it comes to digging a well, gardening and snow removal.

Gardening season for me starts at the end of March, (starting to germinate seeds), and goes into the beginning of November. The lower elevation allows for a longer growing season, and the southern facing slopes on my property receive ample sunlight for orchards and vegetables. Supplying your own food sources is not difficult, as long as you choose your methods and your property wisely.

Other issues to consider are peripheral land features, which I think can be a huge benefit. Earlier I mentioned variety, which is not only the spice of life, but when talking about raw land, also gives you more natural resources. The variety I looked for first was in topography. I wanted a small river, rocks, ridges, draws and meadows. This varied topography gives me more ground, more places for game to hide, and especially a commodity which hardly gets discussed today - privacy! We live in an era where neighbors often don't care about other neighbors, and in our burgeoning surveillance society, many citizens are even being encouraged to spy and snitch on one another like a bunch of tattletales (See Something Say Something…?). Talk about big brother! Whatever happened to minding your own business? So, privacy for many reasons is a hidden treasure. Plus, don't forget that varied topography will always be there offering you privacy even if a fire had gone through. If your trees and vegetation are burned you will always have natural ridges and draws to maintain privacy. I pray fire doesn't happen to anyone, but it is always possible.

Varied topography is as good as gold. Be sure to explore a piece of property thoroughly before buying, and try to get hold of a plat and aerial map of the area, which is an image taken from sky view.

Ridges and draws not only give you variety but more ground as well. They make it possible to keep your home out of sight, and the folds and contours of the land provide more to work with all around. I hope I am repetitive on this part; more varied the topography means fewer major subdivisions around you. (A major subdivision can be hundreds if not thousands of homes while a minor subdivision is not more than five.) This is because it is very difficult to get concentrated septic and drain field approvals on uneven ground.

Now lets think about the "macro equation" of choosing your off grid location. What I mean by macro is the valley or county you reside in which goes beyond the existing acreage that you have purchased. When I say acreage it could be one acre or 50,000; it doesn't matter as long as it is your dream and in your affordability range. (Keep in mind, the smaller the parcel, the higher the probability of having intrusive covenants and regulations). Again, I think that land is way more important than the size of the home. Here in Montana, land parcels vary from a quarter of an acre to 100,000 acres or more. East of the continental divide in Montana, there are a plethora of ranches much larger than the whole valley where I reside. Many of those ranches are 50,000 acres or more. In Northwest Montana, in the valley I live, all of the private land put together consists of only 25,000 acres. The rest of it is National Forest. The northern portion of the county where I live is at least 90% National Forest. The advantages of being surrounded by National Forest are numerous. Remember, in a grid down/collapse scenario or just everyday living, those thousands of acres of forest around you now become your back yard, along with all the resources held within them.

Another reason I chose Northwest Montana was because of its proximity to Western Canada, specifically, Eastern British Colombia and Western Alberta. First of all, I want to share some facts with you about Canada in general. Canada has more than twice our land mass with only 35 million people. Plus, most of their population is concentrated on the eastern part of the country. We have more than eight times their population while at the same time two-thirds of our country is in drought. Speaking of drought, the reason why Canada is a wealthier country than us is because they have so many natural resources. Especially water............. "blue gold". This is why so many countries like China want to trade with Canada. Despite having at least double our land mass, than the lower 48, they only have 250 thousand legal immigrants per year. The US has well over 1 million legal immigrants per year. And who knows how many millions of illegal immigrants arrive. (If amnesty gets passed I've read we could have up to 30 million new residents over night.) Canada will also not allow a US citizen to come in and take a job from a Canadian. WOW!!!!!!! Can you imagine if they did that here? The "dirty dozen" words would be all over the old media. We not only give our jobs away to illegal immigrants but we will pay them not to work. In fact, we will put a little extra icing on the cake and pay for their education and healthcare too. This happens infrequently in Canada.

If Obamacare gets implemented then US companies will have more incentives to hire illegal aliens because they will be exempt from paying into the healthcare system. This will hurt American citizens even more.

I have to admit that Canada is a beautiful country and rich in natural resources. To me the most beautiful place in the world is British Colombia and Western Alberta. In fact, the most beautiful drive I've ever seen is Highway 93, from Eureka, Montana to Jasper, Alberta. I even contacted an attorney to see if I could get dual residency a few years ago. Long story short, the application for dual residency would only be approved if I said that I was about to be hired by a Canadian company. Lie and obtain approval or tell the truth and be denied. I simply couldn't lie about it. Now that I am in my 50's my window of opportunity to move to Canada has been eliminated-they don't want you in Canada full time (year round) if you are too old. Too old is 50 for Canada.

A quick word about Western Montana. As I'm writing this chapter, there is an article that has just been written titled : The Best Places to Relocate in 2013. The first place recommended is Montana. It reads: "The United States is more polarized than ever, divided along ideological lines into regions that may as well be entirely different countries. As if the antics of Washington DC aren't enough, millions of American families are stuck in the political crossfire and wondering where to turn. Some fear an impending collapse, while others simply want to provide a safe and free environment for their children".

"The best option for anyone feeling trapped in a web of government regulation may be to vote with his or her feet. These are the top five states for survivalists and the self-sufficient in 2013, based primarily on population density, sustainability and citizen freedoms." This article mentioned Montana as being the best place to relocate in 2013. The next four states are in the following order: North Dakota, Washington, Utah and then Idaho. Of course, like any other article based on "Best Places," it can be very subjective.

The next paragraph mentions that Montana's weakness is its climate. Personally, I am looking at the glass half full. In Montana, we can dig a hole in a northern slope and store food for a few months out of the year. Just a comparison............ do you remember hurricane Katrina? It got ugly for lots of reasons. One of the main reasons was that food and water became contaminated within a couple days. When refrigeration is gone and the climate is warm, it's a bad combination.

This article also mentions how "Western Montana sees cooler summers, milder winters and gets the majority of the state's rainfall, while the eastern half is arid and cold". I do want to mention that even though eastern Montana has its own beauty, it can also be quite challenging. Some people have a hard time digging a well because the aquifers for digging a well can be few and far between. Even when you successfully "hit" water while drilling, it can often be "undrinkable". I have visited quite a few people who have cisterns and they have to have water delivered. In a time when natural resources are scarce, especially water, Eastern Montana could be a challenge. Eastern Montana also has a lot of high winds. If you are generating electricity via wind then Eastern Montana might be a preferable choice. And speaking of making your own energy, Eastern Montana, because of its high winds, has more sunny days for solar. Again, do your research and find out which place is best depending on your skills, needs, comfort zones and financial situation.

To reiterate, it is vital that your land be at least semi-remote. When I leave the valley I reside in, I have to drive at least 45 minutes to get to the next TOWN. I feel the best place to live in these economic times of uncertainty is where the natural resource to human population ratio is not compromised. This means that you need to take into account the number of people residing in the region for hundreds of miles around. Having a farmstead in rural Pennsylvania may feel like an off-grid retreat, but where do you think all the starving masses from Cincinnati, Pittsburgh, and Philadelphia are going to go if the final shoe drops on the economy? How about New York, L.A. or Atlanta? Those "rural" towns and hills will suddenly feel very cramped and highly uncomfortable for reasons I'm sure you can imagine. I am often asked, why Montana, or, why the Northwest states? Take a look at a population density map of America, and you'll see why.

Next, you need to think about what tangible assets you would get with the land you are interested in. Water, as I've discussed is extremely important. Not just from a survival standpoint but a recreational standpoint as well. Next are trees. Trees do a lot more than just give shade. They deliver nutrients to the soil which benefit the whole ecosystem. They provide cover for animals and are a harvestable renewable resource. With a relatively sizable portion of timber, you can stay warm through the winter for the rest of your life. This is why living in an area that has 90% National Forest Service just ten minutes away is such a benefit.

On my property when I see a tree downed by wind or a tree that has just died from insects, I look at it as "free heat". Do you know what energy is worth these days? Coal plants are being over-regulated and are shutting down all over the country. Do you think energy is going to get cheaper? If your answer is yes, give me a call, I have a bridge to sell you. Being able to provide your own energy of any kind would shave a huge percentage off your cost of living.

Nothing goes to waste on my property. That includes all natural resources, from trees, to wild animals, to goat and chicken droppings; just about everything can be reused or recycled. Another natural tangible asset which should not be overlooked, believe it or not, is the common rock. Just go to a landscape nursery business and see what they charge to harvest, haul and cut stones for building and walkways. The prices are often outrageous!

I have harvested rock to cover berms, cover walkways, border gardens, etc. My daylight basement is covered with river rock which would be at least a $30,000 bill if I had to buy it through a contractor. Yet, I provided it for myself free from my own property. I just picked up a rock here and there over a couple of years and put it in my UTV and away I went. Plus, some of my roads I had to build to code, and I did so by supplying my own base gravel which is also on my property. Needless to say, having these natural resources has saved me a ton of money.

Varied topography also offers the opportunity for a daylight basement to be built-in to a ridge or hillside. This gives your basement greater insulation for temperature and sound. A daylight basement makes a lot of sense. It doubles the square-footage of your home very inexpensively. I recommend putting two large egress windows downstairs in the basement. This will not only add light but give you the ability to convert part of your basement into two more "legal" bedrooms if need be. You never know if you might have to move family members in because of some kind of catastrophe. The more options you have the better, especially if you ever consider re-sale.

Your off-grid land will not only save you money and provide ample resources, it will also give you a chance to finally live healthier. With all the chemicals that are going into city water today, not just fluoride and chlorine but dozens of others as well, drawing your drinking water from a natural source or a well could save you numerous health problems down the road. Do you know how many people pay for city water but still buy bottled water to drink? A lot!!!! Besides, I still don't trust bottled water.

Edible plants also have incredible health properties and an abundance of them should be a prerequisite for any land that you plan to purchase. Also, working the land, in itself, is a great way to stay in shape. I only spend about 30 to 40 minutes per day in the garden but, it beats driving across a huge state every week. (Which I did as a pharmaceutical representative).

Beyond survival, you must also sit back for a moment and think about all the recreation enjoyments and moments of pure wonder that comes from owning a little land. I enjoy foraging and a life of botany which includes edible and medicinal plants, mushrooming and wildflower identification. My property attracts deer, bear, moose, elk and many other critters that I can hunt, or simply watch. And most of all, the area where my homestead resides is an ornithologist's paradise. One of my most beloved hobbies is birdwatching (ornithology). The local riparian zone brings in a lot of exotic birds, especially during breeding season. I wouldn't even know where to begin listing all the varieties of birds because the river draws in dozens if not a hundred different species.

Once you find a property which has all the resources and benefits you are looking for, it is time to make the purchase. This is where most people get tripped up.

First of all, I feel the ONLY debt that should be hanging over anyone's head should be for their land and home. I've seen too many people going into debt for vehicles, furniture, clothing, food, toys, on and on. It's ridiculous! People sink themselves into such meaningless debt every day! It is time for the average American to learn that it is much easier to live below their means than above. If you don't have the cash don't buy it! When you are constantly paying interest, there is no way you can take advantage of time leverage and get ahead. Period. Especially in a disintegrating society where political correctness trumps hard work, effort, proven results and qualifications. Buying good rural land is the only acceptable financial burden worth undertaking, because it is the only investment today that will pay dividends for your retirement. Don't let the money issues frighten you when it comes to buying property for your off-grid or country life. If you ever spend money on anything, it should be this!

Twenty acre parcels or larger are preferable when making a purchase because the zoning laws are typically easier to deal with on a piece that size. In Montana, if you own 20 acres you get what's called agriculture or forest zoning. This means you pay a lot less in property taxes than you would if you own 19.99 acres. If money is tight, go for raw land and worry about the residence later. You can always build a little cabin and add improvements as you go. Many people get frightened by the prospect of building their home from scratch. Suck it up and get over it! You are an off-grid pioneer! This life is not for the meek! Take the process one step at a time, and you'll be surprised how quickly your homestead will come together.

Lots of people ask me what is the perfect size parcel to buy when looking to buy land for a "hobby farm", I say it depends...........on your financial situation, topography and natural resources on the land, etc. It also depends on your interests and hobbies. (Hence, the term "hobby farm".) There are so many considerations ranging from the number of animals you want to the species of animals. Do you want to garden like I have or do you want a commercial farm? Do you want to be able to hunt, fish and trap on it? If I had to pick a number, I would say between 20 and 40 acres if you lived in a valley similar to where I live. What I mean by this is that if you lived in a valley that has millions of acres of National Forest Service in the area. An additional characteristic would be lots of lakes and streams. The purpose of me saying this is so you don't have to travel far to harvest or recreate around natural resources. Living near natural resources will someday not just be for quality-of-life but could be for survival reasons as well. If it's flat, I would want more land around me to buffer myself (privacy.) Plus, remember, less varied topography means less places for wild animals to hide. I like my wildlife!

Also, keep in mind, that the size of your house determines the cost of your taxes, insurance and maintenance. If I'm not redundant on some of these important facts, shame on me. This alone has been enough to destroy many families and kick them out of there homes. Our "banksters" here in America have been using fractional reserve lending forever. Basically, they are lending out 10 times the money they have on hand with no real money or accountability to back it up. But, they want you to finance all the newest regulations on your land, right from the start. This can include septic and drain fields, wells, foundations to codes, driveway and roads, electricity............. Wouldn't it be nice if your bank would finance your land, with a minimal down payment, and you could make improvements on it as you had the money? That's called living below your means. This is the way America was initially built and there was a lot less foreclosures.

Don't forget to keep track of your amortization schedule. This is the breakdown of interest and principal on any loans you take out. It shows you, on every payment from first to last, a breakdown of how much interest and principal you pay every month. Most banks don't volunteer to give them out..........the dumber you are the more interest you pay. Banks love this system. This is a big reason why 90% of Americans are in urban America and often stuck there. Too many people are either under water in their loans and in too many cases are losing their homes. Remember that after rent/mortgage, taxes and insurance, most Americans use most of their disposable income to pay for food, energy and recreation/entertainment. The hobby farm/self sufficient lifestyle gives you an opportunity to dovetail all three together with little cost.

Unfortunately, most banks don't give a damn about you, and will rarely provide you with even an amortization schedule. (But, they are getting better these days because the public is demanding it). Unless you request one, they rarely give you one at the time of closing. The more interest you pay, the more likely they are to sell that loan for a good buck (example of derivatives). I do a lot of financial counseling for people on a volunteer basis and I can't tell you how many folks are unaware of these facts. It's a real shame because these people actually thought they had equity in their homes and it turned out they were "underwater" in their loans. Not much legitimacy there! Speaking of legitimacy, I'm sure you've heard of the 700 TRILLION dollars we have in derivatives? Most of this is "packaged up" notes of real estate which is just fake paper dollars with little value that has been bundled and re-bundled and re-sold. Not much tangibility there.

I also recommend you try to find landowners who have the ability to think "outside the box." This will give you more opportunities to buy outside normal restrictions. For example, when I sell a piece of land, I try and find like-minded individuals. People who have different skills who are willing to work as a community if need be. Some of my skills involve hunting, butchering, fishing, trapping, gardening, medicinal plants, edible plants, some alternative energy and much more. In an economy that could come crashing down on all of us, those who have the ability and desire to use forgotten 19th-century skills and dovetail them with 21st century technology will be in demand. (Do you think my three college degrees are really worth anything? I've got another bridge to sell you). That said, none of us can do this alone and community is essential. If you are able to combine all these factors into a single, well-planned land purchase, then you have just made an investment that you will never in your life regret.

A good book for reference: Strategic Relocation, North American Guide to safe Places. 3rd edition. By Joel Skousen and Andrew Skousen.

Chapter 8: Choosing And Building Your Off Grid Home

It seems quite evident to me, and market behavior supports my view, that rural land is going to be much more valuable than a home in urban or suburban America. So if you want to be out in the country and as self-sufficient as possible, owning land that complements whatever home you decide to build should be your number one consideration.

When I was researching which home to build for my homesteading project, I looked at just about everything. I looked into manufactured homes, stick built homes, timber frame and log homes. Today they even make insulated Yurts that costs a fraction of what traditional homes cost. There are also cordwood style homes, straw bale homes, earth homes-it's up to you to do some research.

Considerations for myself included "the country feel", the insulation factor, the structural integrity, the resale value, and of course the looks. Looks are always personal and subjective and obviously the utility of the property should be made a priority over whether or not it is as "pretty" as we might like. There were pros and cons to each style of building and I made a list to help discern which would best fit my needs.

Manufactured Homes
These days manufactured homes are much better built than their older cousin "the trailer." When I started my equity building in the early 1980s back in New York, I started with a trailer in a trailer park. It was the only equity that I felt was worth purchasing because of the small amount of money I had. This way I knew I could establish some equity and yet still have a buffer, because of the small payments, from being put out in the street because of bad and unpredictable times. Today, manufactured homes are built exceptionally well and can still be brought to your land on wheels. The company will put the pieces together on your property when they arrive. They often include wood stoves, vaulted ceilings, multiple bathrooms, and are totally finished from floor to ceiling.

The biggest benefit of a manufactured home is probably the price per square foot. Just like a typical stick frame house, they vary in price depending on the builder and materials, but generally the costs are much cheaper because they build many copies of one style home. However, these homes also come with their cons. Most people would think that the number one con would be the stigma, but frankly, no one should care what other people think. My father always told me that unless "those people" are paying your taxes and mortgage, their opinion should mean squat. In other words, whoever is paying the mortgage and taxes should make the decisions. If your number one consideration is price then you should make that a priority, but keep in mind this choice can also negatively affect your resale value.

I feel the two main cons of a manufactured home are lending and covenants. Regarding lending, some banks will not loan money on these homes. If they do, you usually need to install a foundation that meets strict county and state codes. Covenants can vary from property to property, meaning each individual landowner will most likely have their own. Not to mention, there are also zoning laws which could affect your options on a manufactured home. If you can find land where there are no covenants, no zoning, a big enough parcel for privacy, and a reasonable elevation…buy it! And by a reasonable elevation, I mean less than 3500 feet, especially if you prefer less snow and longer growing seasons. By the way, I do know some people living my lifestyle at over 5,000 feet of elevation, they just have longer winters. If you have a snow mobile, snow shoes or cross country skies you could be in heaven. Go where your hobbies and interests are!

Stick And Timber Homes
When dealing with stick frame and timber homes it's all personal preference. Timber homes are going to be more expensive because of the labor and the scribed beams. Each gives you the opportunity to control how much insulation you want to put between your inside and outside walls. The price of a stick frame home can vary extensively with square footage, bathrooms and plumbing in general, vaulted ceilings, how many floors, how many angles (for example: dormers), doors, windows, siding such as wood, hardy plank, vinyl, etc. (Hardy plank has the least maintenance because it is a concrete product but is one of the most expensive sidings). What is nice about a stick frame home is that you can build something small and add-on as your fiscal situation improves. (Most people don't do this but they should.)

Last, but not least, the cost of the builder himself must be considered. I prefer a builder who thinks outside the box. Especially, in regards to lending and payment schedules. It's also important that you put in the contract a time of completion and a penalty clause in case the house isn't completed on time. Make sure that the builder shows up every day and on time for at least eight hours. The last thing you want to be is a babysitter.

Another major consideration is of lending. Are you going to try and get a construction loan, pay cash, or negotiate a payment plan with the builder and/or landowner? If your money is tight, then I would put more emphasis on a small home and a greater emphasis on a large piece of land. This usually trips people up, don't buy the most you can afford, buy what you can very comfortably afford. A smart man would rather live in a Teepee on a nice size piece of private land than live in a 5000 ft.^{2} home in the middle of some town that might restrict his building with covenants and regulations. I know of so many people who live with too many regulations, it's ridiculous. Some property owners, especially in subdivisions, can't even cut down a tree or some have to even plant them as per covenants. Some owners can't put in a fire pit or even a vegetable garden in their front yard or an "out building" or if they do, it has to be a certain distance from your neighbors boundary. I can probably add another 500 examples of ridiculous regulations I have heard of over the last several years. Is this freedom to you? Plus, having this location can possibly become a danger zone during a crisis.

My personal choice after all of my research was to go with the log cabin method. The sturdiness and insulation properties were fantastic, and maintenance is minimal.

Location And Style

When choosing a building site, the first thing I looked for was a small ridge or hillside to establish a daylight basement. I can't stress enough the importance of having a daylight basement. First, it doubles the square footage of your building for a very reasonable price. You can use this space for anything, but a root cellar is highly valuable, especially to the off-grid lifestyle. Daylight basements maintain very cool temperatures, even in summer, and help preserve food you have set aside for the next month, or the next year.

My next consideration was the position of the home and whether it gave comfort. I positioned my cabin north, northwest. I did this because of the fact that, two houses ago, the house where I lived for 15 years, was positioned S.W. It was so hot in the summer I could barely live in it. Thank God that house had a daylight basement to live in during the summer. Just remember it takes a lot more energy to cool a home than to heat one. (We are lucky here in Montana since nights and mornings are always nice and cool and almost never humid.) A coziness and country feel may seem like secondary concerns, but never forget this is your home, and will most likely be your home for a long time. If you do not find solace in the surroundings you have chosen, this can negatively affect your mental state, and interfere with everything you do on a daily basis. I personally enjoy the rustic look, so after I made my decision to go with a log cabin, there was no turning back.

Cabin chinking (a paste used to cement the cracks in between logs) made today can last for decades, where as in the past, you had to re-chink every 10 years. In a cabin I can hammer a nail anywhere I want (that is huge for me!). I hate drywall with a passion! In a standard home, it's not just the labor of putting up drywall, taping it, pasting it, sanding it and painting it but also the fact that every time you put a nail in it, you have to spackle and re-paint when you move that nail. To be able to avoid this annoyance is fantastic!

For flooring, I went to a lumberyard and purchased one by eight boards, and simply glued and screwed them down to the sub-floor. It looks great and very rustic. I used Aspen in the kitchen area and fir and larch throughout the rest of the cabin. I used an open floor plan just like a typical hunting lodge, and maintenance of the floor is quick and easy; we just mop with tung oil once a year…and that's it! We never have to do any sanding and if a scratch scars the floor we dab on a little tung oil and it's gone. Voilà!

Further Considerations

There are a lot of peripheral considerations when taking on a building project:

Proximity to a clean water source (aquifer) and well digging costs. Heating and cooling, space for livestock, fencing and security fire zones and flood zones. Septic and sanitation, space for your electrical generator, battery banks, and solar panels. Space for a sustainable garden that will feed you and your family all year round. Proximity to friendly neighbors or necessary distance from unfriendly neighbors. Varied terrain that gives ample privacy just to name a few…

One issue I take seriously is resale value. One thing no one can predict is the future, but you can establish your property in such a way as to make it valuable regardless of good or bad economic circumstances. My research showed me that log homes sell extremely well, especially in northwest Montana where I reside. Some people assume that log homes are extra maintenance. I think just the opposite, and the overall value of properties with log buildings today speaks for itself. I will stain the outside about every five years and call it good.

Building a loft and cathedral ceilings can give your home a more open look. Functionally, they allow for heat to rise to the upper floor with greater ease. If your bedroom is upstairs in the loft you can stop feeding your wood stove (or what ever heat source you use) earlier in the day, and still remain comfortable through the night. I usually stop feeding my wood stove around 3 o'clock on an average winter day because it can get too hot to sleep.

Decks or porches are mandatory. Whether it be for storage, relaxing or just to have an extension of home. I love the covered porch because we don't have to shovel snow off the deck anymore. I had to do this in one of my previous homes and I hated it. To me it is tedious work, that is also why I don't mow or rake anymore either. (Except around my raised beds because the goats are not allowed in the vegetable garden area).

As for electricity, I enjoy making my own. To me it's like picking a tomato in my garden or harvesting a deer or elk and having it for dinner. In other words, it's so much fun to make, grow, harvest, build or gather the things I need to live. I have a small solar array which gives me enough energy for eight months of easy living. For about four months of the year I supplement my solar array with a generator. Having a generator near your home is very important. I live quite well and have some modern electronic items at my disposal with minimal effort in terms of electricity production.

Another factor for a log home is light. Because you don't have white drywall all over the house the "light factor" can be an issue. This is why I prefer an open floor plan in my log cabin. (In other words, I don't have a bunch of little rooms all over the place). The open floor plan and loft gives me plenty of light for daytime activities.

For bathroom and sanitation concerns, I have made it extremely simple. We do have an outhouse that we use on a regular basis, but we also have a indoor toilet that we flush with a bucket of water. (Don't tell anybody we have an indoor toilet. It will ruin my "bad ass mountain man" reputation). I put in a regulation septic and drain field because it makes sense to do this for resale value and it's inexpensive to do so. My cabin is plumbed for three bathrooms even though I do not use all of those features.

Where I live in Northwest Montana it is legal to have an outhouse if you own 20 acres or more. Some counties have different regulations than others. So in other words, 20 acres will give you fewer regulations, lower property taxes and a greater quality of life. (This is because 20 acres will give you "forest" or "agriculture" zoning.) If you can afford 20 acres, I would recommend it. I would rather get the acreage and live with an outhouse until my fiscal situation improved instead of getting a smaller piece of land and putting extra money into taxed infrastructure. But that is a personal decision that you will have to make depending on your financial situation. If you're not zoned for an outhouse you could always disguise it with something like a "tool shed" so you can have emergency bathroom facilities, just in case!

I chose to not have any interior pipes for incoming water. I can literally say that I have no "traditional" running water in my home. In Alaska, they call this a "dry cabin". Not many people in America would want to make this sacrifice. In fact, when I shower I use a solar shower bag that I hang over the tub. It holds 4 gallons of water and I can buy one at any camping department store for $15. Some skeptics might reel in horror at a home without interior pipes or municipal water. Some might even call it a fire hazard. In reality, according to the insurance company statistics, there is much more likelihood of WATER DAMAGE to their homes than fire damage in this country. Log homes are extremely fire resistant, so the chances of a blaze catching is minute. (Plus, I have taken away all trees that could fall on my cabin and we even have fire extinguishers in every area of the cabin.) Suburban "McMansions" suffer from broken pipes, bursting toilets, malfunctioning dishwashers and flooded washrooms all the time. Interior piping is not necessary for a home to function and it presents the constant risk of water and mold damage. Good luck trying to sell a home with toxic mold and mildew problems. I've heard of banks, who own foreclosed, non-occupied homes, paying off home inspectors to overlook mold and mildew damage. Beware.

Such ignorant presumptions about off grid living are common. It's not because most Americans are spoiled but because they don't know better and they haven't been around this type of living. What they see as a major inconvenience is actually a very inexpensive and different method; I use a 200 gallon water tank in the loft which gravity feeds the kitchen faucet in my cabin. I use only a short seven foot piece of pex piping. The only inconvenience is having to fill the tank with a garden hose, from my well, and it only takes about 30 minutes every eight to twelve days. Much more convenient, I would say, than having to worry about whether I remembered to pay an overpriced monthly water bill full of chemicals.

Off-Grid Is Simply Better
Sadly, most Americans are renters, and they cling to a renter's mindset. The largest subset of people who are actually homeowners are people who live in subdivisions. Most of them have always lived on city water

and sewer, and do not realize they have a choice in the matter. Though they own a home, they still live like renters, constantly making payments to one corporate entity or another just to receive the necessities that allow them to survive.

The system doesn't help much either. In fact, the system goes out of its way to discourage Americans from building off-grid. Most banks will not lend capital for a home unless you have hookups to a well, septic, electricity and meet other county codes and regulations. They allow and sometimes even encourage the misconceptions about offgrid construction. This can sometimes be remedied by giving your lender at least a 30% down payment. Though the idea might seem frightening to some, I enjoy living off the grid very much. The standard definition of living off grid is "not being hooked up to corporate electricity", which does not really do service to the many changes that are involved in the transition. That said, once you become used to the new way in which you will live day-to-day, I personally feel people will find this lifestyle is much simpler and easier than the modern grind we have been conditioned to accept. My girlfriend often says that she would rather work at home "doing hobbies" we enjoy then working for an employer. And this is coming from someone who works part-time, loves her job, and has a great employer.

I also fear that many options available to the working middle class in America are going to quickly disappear. It is very important that we all begin to think creatively, and outside what the system deems "normal" if we are to thrive or even survive. If money is scarce, don't be afraid to look for like-minded people and share the purchase of land and even a home, if necessary. Remember that the building portion of your home is the most financially and emotionally challenging part of the homesteading process. Don't give up when things get a little tough.

When I say look for like minded people, look for people with similar goals and dreams. Individually, buying land for some people can be overwhelming, but together with friends and/or family your dreams can come true. Each person doesn't even have to come in with equal money/capital to make this new lifestyle materialize. For example, the one with the highest amount of capital invested can be the leader. Or other investors or owners can invest more time or skills into land projects. One could be knowledgeable in building, gardening, alternative energy, animals, hunting/fishing/trapping, nutrition and one could have a job working at home on the internet to create cash flow. Maybe, one could stay behind full time and be a caretaker while others are getting their final "ducks in a row" in the city. Remember, one of the words I hope I have been redundant on-synergy? Communicate, negotiate and create a plan of action. Then put everything agreed upon in writing in contract form, so nobody whines down the road.

Right now, too many Americans are buying homes in cookie-cutter subdivisions because realtors are telling them the value is great and that the market has hit bottom. This may be possible to swallow if the only thing you're considering is the economy at the moment. But if you are thinking about the future, about self-sufficiency, functionality, privacy, wild game, room for domestic animals, acreage, your personal lifestyle and dream, you may want to reconsider the traditional consumerist route.

Living below your means, knowing the fine line between needs and wants, being self-sufficient, and having fun in nature every day is a vast switch from what we are often told the "American Dream" is supposed to be. I say forget the propaganda, and live as free as possible. Nothing could be more American than the off-grid life. Think homesteading and pioneering and doing everything your way instead of inheriting someone else's problems.

Chapter 9: Hunting, fishing and trapping

The primary reason I came to Montana at the age of 26 was for the hunting and fishing adventures. I have always been attracted by everything in nature and everything natural. The natural world made sense while the rest of our consumerist corporatist culture felt fake and phoney. It was all a distraction from what was really important. In fact, corporate America was my means to the end for me to get my "hobby farm" and live off the land.

In my 27 years of living in Montana I would say that 99.9% of all meat and fish I have eaten has been wild game. The only exceptions are when I have eaten at restaurants or someone else's home, or domestic animals I've raised on my own land for consumption.

In Montana, we can hunt every month of the year, except July and August, if you're a bow hunter, spring bear and turkey hunter, and a "cat" hunter (mountain lions and bobcats). This does not include some of the smaller game and varmints that you can hunt year round. It's an outdoorsman's paradise!

This chapter might be pretty boring for the average Montanan to read, since the life I'm describing here regarding hunting and fishing is definitely not out of the norm. This chapter, like most of this book, would be more appreciated by the many people who reside in urban/suburban America but are cradling a similar dream of immersing themselves in the off-grid or just country lifestyle. I would like in particular to speak to the numerous American hunters and fishermen out there who have immeasurable passion and enthusiasm for the outdoors. I want to talk to the person who doesn't want to follow the masses of "sheeple"; the person who is desperate not to become one of those hamsters running on their treadmills to nowhere; those people who have not experienced self-sufficiency and outdoor adventure.

I've been very blessed with a lot of good luck in the woods but, I put in my time! I came here to hunt and fish and oh boy that is indeed what I have done! Conservatively, I have harvested more than 170 plus big-game animals on the Northwest part of this continent, and the great majority have come from Montana. I can also say that approximately 85% of what I have harvested has been with a bow and arrow. Ironically, if I had been employed by the National Forest Service in my early 20's (as I so dearly wanted) I probably wouldn't have harvested so many animals. I would have most likely been in the wildlife division and would have been very satisfied trapping live animals and reading nature's signs in the forest. It's a shame when I see so many National Forest Service workers who got their jobs through affirmative action and have absolutely no passion and enthusiasm for the outdoors. They just took the job because of the high paycheck and pension, what a shame!

One of my personal goals, when I came to this great state, was to harvest at least one of each of the 13 species of big-game that walk on Montana soil. I had to go to Northwest territories to harvest my caribou and to British Columbia for my wolves, (Today however, we can now legally hunt and trap wolves in Montana.) The last of the 13 species to harvest for my goal to be complete was a grizzly bear, so I went to Alaska for this hunt. I was successful and took a grizzly by shooting him in the heart at 175 yards with a 300 Weatherby. He "piled up" in 30 yards. Here in Northwest Montana we do have plenty of grizzly bears and an occasional mountain caribou strolling by. Unfortunately, they are strictly protected and cannot be hunted despite the fact that the grizzly's quite common. Hunting a grizzly bear is, of course, considered "politically incorrect." I'm sure you've never heard that term before in America!

The 13 species of big game I have harvested are: whitetail deer, mule deer, elk, black bear, grizzly bear, caribou, wolf, mountain lion, moose, bighorn sheep, mountain goat, buffalo and antelope. I've tracked and hunted them all and it's been a great ride! The big reason I have harvested so many animals is because of the fact that Montana has masses of whitetail deer, especially in the western part. My first 19 years here, I lived in the central west part of Montana.

There are three major rivers that run through the central part of this region: The Clark Fork, Bitterroot and the Blackfoot. Along these river bottom areas sit many homes and roads. Years ago before I arrived, the Montana fish and game department made these areas open to bow hunting ONLY. The reason for the designation was two fold: so that many homes, vehicles, and people in general wouldn't get hit from stray bullets, and, as was told to me by an employee at the Fish and Game Department, these areas were used for a "seed" crop of deer. They made it very clear to me, especially with bow hunting, that there is an 80 percent rule. In other words, 20% of the bow hunters harvest 80% of the deer. It may even be a 90-10 ratio. I think every valley should have a bow hunting ONLY area just for the "seed" crop aspect. I was also told that there are more deer in these areas than hunters could ever harvest. Unfortunately, there are so many deer in these areas that more deer were getting killed by vehicles than by bow hunters, as per the Fish and Game Department.

Bow hunting has a much lower success rate than rifle hunting, by far.

In Montana, on specific river bottom areas, bow hunters can harvest up to seven whitetail deer a year/season. Years ago, you could also harvest mule deer with B tags but no more. In these areas a Montana bow hunter can harvest up to five whitetail does with a B tag, and one whitetail buck with an A tag. There are also special lottery drawings, and winners can receive an extra B tag for another buck. As you can imagine this is a bow hunter's paradise. During my time there I have harvested well over 100 whitetail deer and donated at least 50% of the meat to folks who appreciate it.

Today I am in my 50s and have definitely mellowed out regarding time spent hunting and fishing. Back in my 20's and 30s, I would hunt every minute that I could get out in the field. Now I am not as active but I still give it a good try. I don't like to be a quitter! Now that it's later in life for me, I try to hunt where I can drive close to my kill. Otherwise, I'll need someone to help me pack in and pack out. This "game" only gets heavier as the years pass.

I hunt with moderation and modifications to deal with my aging spine. This serves me well and, as I have observed, 98% of men put big-game hunting on the back burner when they reach approximately 55 years of age. That is to say, their passion and enthusiasm for big-game hunting diminishes greatly, plus they eat a lot less meat at this age. They might go on a random guided or local hunt, but they do it only occasionally. They do not "live to hunt, or hunt to live" anymore. As I am rapidly approaching the end of my "adventure years", I can say that I have definitely lived my dream. It was not easy getting to Montana or staying here, so I don't take one minute for granted and live every day like it's my last. Despite all my difficulties with affirmative action/quotas/political correctness and my declining health, I still feel very blessed!

In a way, we almost do things backwards, don't we? Wouldn't it be great if we all went into a semi-retirement at the age of say, 35? We could have a little money set aside and maybe be out of debt. Then we can hunt and fish to our heart's content until we are about 55 or 60. Then go back to work if we financially need to..........depending on your lifestyle and investment choices. If you observe people, especially American men, they rarely achieve many longstanding goals after they retire at age 60, usually because they are too overweight, tired or sick. Too many of them just die when they retire. It's a shame! I have even found that a lot of men go back to work after retirement simply because they are bored and feel as though they are wasting away. So, my message here is do what you can while you can. Go for it! Cultivate your interests and hobbies especially if they assist in keeping you healthy and give you joy. None of us are owed another day nor are we guaranteed good health. I thought I would be working out in the gym until my 80's.....my spine told me I was wrong.

Hunting Methods

I don't want people to think I'm "anti-gun," because that is not the case at all. But, I really enjoy the challenge of bow hunting. I enjoy the fact that archery hunting in the woods is very low impact and because I wear camouflage, it's very rare that anyone ever sees me. I like being in the woods when I can be part of the landscape. I notice every bird and mammal that flies or walks by. I notice every species of tree, shrub and wild flower that is around me and take in all the glory of nature.

I would say that 50% of what I have harvested with a bow has been from a tree stand, though my ability to sit still very long has definitely diminished these days. I have to sit, stand, stretch, twist and do a few exercises while in the stand, and this does sometimes draw attention to my presence.

When on the ground, I never position myself in a spot unless I can see at least 50 yards in order to prepare a shot. If that is not the case I make sure I have higher ground so I can hear something coming (sound travels up easier). I concentrate on looking at only a few specific trails that are up wind. Then, I know when to be absolutely still and quiet before the animal approaches. If a whitetail deer approaches, even one you don't want to harvest, and it finds out you are there, your hunt is often over. You can give yourself away by movement, sound or scent and every animal in the forest is good at picking out inconsistencies in their environment. Remember, you're hunting in their living room.

When bow hunting, I enjoy the longer days, the elk rut, the warmer weather and fewer hunters breathing down my neck. (Bow season opens the first weekend in September.) Bow hunters in general are often more experienced hunters. Just about everyone starts by hunting with a gun and then some graduate to a bow and arrow. I'm a firm believer that everyone should learn to walk before they run. I'm not taking any sides or saying that gun hunting takes less skill, but I am saying you better know what you're doing when you're hunting with a "pointy stick" and trying to kill something at 40 yards or less.

Regarding rifle hunting, people often ask me what caliber rifle they should get when starting out, and I always tell them it depends on what they are trying to accomplish. For different jobs you need different tools.

For example, the 30-06 has been around for a long time, it is a very powerful 30 caliber rifle, and accommodates a wide variety of loads compared to most rifles; you can purchase a lot of different grain bullets for this gun. It gives you the versatility to hunt different types of game depending on the size of your bullet and powder. If you don't reload, you can buy many different factory grain loads.

However, in Eastern Montana the 30-06 is usually not the best choice because of the greater shot distances required in that region. The open plains of eastern Montana would do better with a more flat shooting gun like a 7 MM or a .270. Many people in Western Montana also prefer the 7MM or .270 for certain hunting situations.

If you're into varmint hunting, which would include coyotes, fox, badgers, gophers etc, (which you can hunt year round in Montana.) I would recommend a .223 or a .222. Anything larger, even a .243, might do the job but would leave very little fur because of rather large exit holes. For "gophers", which are called Columbian ground squirrels, on my property I use a .22 caliber. If you have a garden, you need to keep these critters down to a dull roar or they will eat you out of house and home.

I have harvested my share of cottontail and snowshoe rabbits, which you can also hunt year round. I have even harvested some pheasant, ducks and geese, but by far my favorite small game animal to harvest in Montana is the mountain grouse. I have harvested plenty of Sharp tail, Hungarian Partridge and Sage grouse in the central and eastern part of the state as well but the mountain grouse are the most fun to hunt, and the tastiest.

There are three different species of mountain grouse here in Western Montana. First, is the Ruffed Grouse. This grouse is the most common, fastest in flight and the most tasty by far. The Ruffed Grouse is a beautiful bird that has two different color phases-gray and red (best noticed on his tail). I have Ruffed Grouse all over my property. In the spring they are truly a pleasure and privilege to have around your home. Sometimes, from as early as late January through the spring, they will "drum" (the males will beat their wings against their body to attract mates and defend territories). The meat of the Ruffed Grouse is the most white and the least "gamie" tasting.

My next favorite mountain grouse to harvest is the Blue Grouse. It's meat is also on the white side and very good eating. The Blue Grouse is the largest of the mountain grouse. In the spring, when calling a mate, it will make a "foghorn" type sound that you can hear from a long distance away.

The last species of mountain grouse is the Franklin Grouse. These grouse are the smallest and probably the most rare in the state of Montana. Their meat is on the red side and are a bit more "gamie" in taste than the other two grouse. Keep in mind this is subjective and other people's opinion might differ. One thing I have to say about the Franklin Grouse is that the mature adult males are so beautiful. They are mostly black with mottled white spots and a gorgeous red eyebrow over both eyes. The local name for the Franklin Grouse is the "fools hen". They are very easy to harvest and I have even clubbed a few for lunch. Most of the mountain grouse I have taken in western Montana have been with my bow and arrow. I just enjoy the challenge.

When bow hunting, know your shot limitations. I can hit a pie plate at 50 yards on a regular basis, however, when you shoot past 40 yards, Murphy's law starts to kick you in the butt. The animal could very well hear the twang of your string at that distance and move fast enough to get away. Your shot could end up being a disaster. I have had whitetail deer move so fast that they have ducked my arrow at 25 yards. So be cognizant of your bow shots. (By the way, it doesn't really matter which compound bow you shoot today because the technology has made them all superior to yesterday.)

With a gun, the bullet can create so much shock power that the animal may not go far. When killing a big-game animal with an arrow, you are killing by hemorrhage. An arrow has very little shocking power. In fact, I have killed many an animal with an arrow and they didn't even know they were hit. I've had them just walk away like nothing has happened and suddenly they "pile up". Most bow hunters today are using graphite arrows. These arrows are light and quick but unfortunately they have lost a little kinetic energy. The larger aluminum and wood arrows of the past were heavier and had greater penetration even though they were slower. So, when taking a far shot, you need to take this into consideration because there's a good chance you will wound your animal and never see it again. It's true that in the wild nothing goes to waste. There are plenty of predators out there, but why have the animal suffer and you get short changed from the best meat in the world?

For many years now, I have not been as excited about "the kill." In a way it's even anti-climatic. For me, it's about getting outside, the preparation, the stalk, the challenge, the shot, and of course, the icing on the cake, the excellent meat.

Outdoor Gear Suggestions

As far as hunting gear in general, I can write a book on this topic alone. But, for the sake of this book I will try and be brief. New synthetic clothing has made hunting much easier and more comfortable. For example, polar fleece is not just warm, it is also very quiet compared to older materials. Plus, if it gets wet you can squeeze it dry like a sponge. When hunting in September and October, I wear very light weight clothing because if you sweat when bow hunting and your trying to get close to an animal, good luck. As I mentioned above, synthetic clothing like polar fleece is the most I will wear. When rifle hunting or trapping in late November through February, I will "layer up" with mostly synthetic or wool clothing. These are good choices because if they get wet from sweat, falling in a creek, or it's snowing, I can still stay warm. The best advice to give is to not use cotton! Just never forget that cotton kills. I don't mean to be morbid but cotton has virtually no insulation factor once it gets wet. If you're out in the bush, it's raining and you're stuck spending the night in the woods (which I have) and you're wearing cotton, you're in trouble. You better make sure you have the ability to light a fire and dry your clothes or you will be fighting hypothermia all-night.

Make sure you have a good set of matches, preferably waterproof, to start a fire. I also recommend going to an outdoors/camping store and buying a product called "fire paste"; it's packaged in a tube like toothpaste that you can squirt onto some dry sticks. This product is so flammable that you can light it on top of a rock. I recommend you triple bag this product, especially if you're hunting, in order to keep the scent down to a minimum.

Boots! Very important! When bow hunting in September and October, I do not worry about keeping warm. All I'm concerned with is keeping my human scent down, so I wear rubber boots with little or no insulation that are quiet when walking. Later in the season, November through February, I will wear insulated rubber boots, such as those made by Sorrel or Lacrosse. I recommend winter boots with liners that can be pulled off and easily dried by a fire.

As far as undergarments, shirts, and pants, I just recommend keeping away from cotton. Remember cotton kills. There are so many modern fabrics today that can keep us warm; the best ones, again, are synthetics and wools. Choose the clothing that best suits your climate and personal cold tolerance.

I also recommend always carrying a small first aid kit, a knife and a pair of decent binoculars when hunting in the woods. There are literally hundreds of these tools on the market to fit any budget and desired functionality. Personally, I have never owned an expensive pair of binoculars because I usually beat them up in the woods. A pair of binoculars can come in handy, not just for scouting but for retrieving your game. Many times, after a shot, I have walked very slowly through the woods with a pair of binoculars to locate my downed animal.

Trapping

In Montana and B.C we are also able to trap. I have trapped coyotes, bobcat, red fox, cross fox, beaver, badger, pine marten, mink, ermine, muskrat, skunk, otter, wolverine, raccoon, wolf, silver fox, lynx and possum (back in N.Y.). I actually started trapping in ninth-grade. I trapped in little areas like buffer zones of schools, roads, and other spots where there were small wooded sections around the metropolitan areas of New York City.

These days no one traps for money. They may in some parts of Alaska and Canada but, in the US, it's for the gas money, the outdoor recreation, and the heritage. There may be very few exceptions to that rule these days. For me, trapping requires the most skill and knowledge of any of the outdoor disciplines and recreations. Each trap and set is designed for a specific target animal. For example, I prefer to use snare traps over leg holds for canines (like coyotes, which are incredibly smart). Coyotes have not only a great sense of smell but they also have a "sixth sense." I have caught my share of coyotes in leg hold traps but they are a lot less wary of snare traps.

I've had incredible adventures while trapping out in the woods. One time having a raccoon wrapped it's arms around my legs and tried to bite through my waders; another time a grizzly bear stole my bobcat bait on December 15th at almost 6,000 feet of elevation. The reason I mentioned the grizzly is because most of them are in hibernation by early December.

Ever hear the story about the sly old fox? Foxes are actually very easy to trap; coyotes on the other hand, are much tougher. I have found that wolves are even easier to trap than coyotes. More coyotes are caught simply because there are more of them out there. It's analogous to deer. Whitetail deer are much more intelligent than mule deer, so there are more whitetail because they are smarter. Montana is the only state in which Mule deer are an over the counter tag. In every other state mule deer requires a drawing in order to hunt. In other words they have special regulations to protect the mule deer.

And, just to be clear, I don't care about the political "incorrectness" of trapping. Too many people comment on things they don't understand and have never attempted. Just a quick note about hunting ethics. You sometimes hear (but, it's very rare) that some bonehead kills an animal, leaves the meat, and just takes the horns. We all owe it to the animal that we harvest to make sure we take as much of the meat as required by law.

Hunting Alone Or In Groups

I actually enjoy hunting alone, because when you hunt with someone else, your success is usually entirely dependent on the skill and work ethic of your guide or hunting partner. Unfortunately, I have been on a few guided bow hunts that really turned me off. I mentioned earlier in the book that hunting and fishing has turned into a rich man's game and have become big business. I have seen too many people on guided hunts who should NOT be in the woods. That is to say, they have too much money and not enough hunting skill or even ethics to be out there, and eventually muck up the works for the rest of us.

I have seen bow hunters make multiple missed shots during their short hunting week. I have seen them take shots that are way too far, that are "quartering to" (when an animal is facing the hunter at any angle where the shoulder bone is blocking the heart-lung area) or just trying to squeeze a shot through such thick brush that would make a rifleman hesitate. This is a very unethical shot to take with a bow because the odds of retrieving this animal is extremely slim. This is a waste of good meat and no animal should die such a slow death because of a misplaced shot. The only two shots a bow hunter should take is a broadside shot or a "quartering away" shot. A quartering away shot is the opposite of a "quartering to" shot. This is the shot where the animal is slightly past you and his vital organs, heart and lungs are exposed. In other words, you're shooting your arrow through the back end of the ribs or sometimes even further back in order to penetrate the heart-lung area. This shot will give you a high probability of a quick kill because there are no major bones to penetrate like a shoulder bone.

Remember, a bow and arrow does not have the shocking power that a rifle bullet has when killing. Big-game animals are way tougher than us frail humans. I've tracked animals for a few hundred yards and been amazed by how little of a blood trail they have left even though I had made a very good shot. 90% of my animals pile up within 100 yards.

Because of the numerous novice mistakes made during such events, guided hunts are often overrated. In too many cases the guide doesn't care about equal opportunities for each hunter. If the hunter is wealthy and can afford a big tip the guide often doesn't even care about him taking unethical "quartering to" shots. I've seen guides looks the other way after a client bow hunter takes an unethical shot, it's usually because he's wealthy........ what do you call that? I guess it's possible return business.

I don't want to give you the impression that I have not wounded any animals, it happens. When you have hunted as much game as I have over this many years, there will be a few regrets. It hurts greatly to not retrieve an animal and I don't know of too many hunters who have killed over 20 animals that have not wounded at least one of them.

One nice thing about rifle hunting is the fact that you can take "quartering to" shots, if you use a good 30 caliber rifle. Here in Montana rifle hunting is often done with at least some snow on the ground and this makes tracking a whole lot easier. The key is to do your best to ensure the animal does not suffer.

Hunting alone has its disadvantages too, like being forced to carry a kill by yourself as well as being forced to stay hyper-alert for other predators that might see your game as an easy lunch, but the work is always worth it. Hunting alone removes all the extra uncertainties, noises, smells, and dangers of untrained partners. My girlfriend Karen has called me in a few elk that I have harvested with a bow and it was a great time, so there are some exceptions to the rule.

Wild Game Preparation And Taste

People ask me all the time what is the best tasting big-game meat? First of all, I have to say it's a subjective answer. In other words, every hunter or connoisseur who is lucky enough to dine on wild game has a different opinion. Personally, for me it is a tossup between Moose, elk and antelope, though a lot of people might not agree with the antelope part. I find antelope to be like sushi; half the people love it and half turn their noses up. To me, regardless of the species of game, the key is taking care of the meat in the proper way. This should be your number one consideration as a hunter.

For years now, especially since we don't use a freezer, I have been boning out my meat in the field. I will always have a game bag ready to go, unless I'm with an outfitter/guide that does the work for me. When the animal is down on the ground I start by gutting him out immediately. Bow hunters or anyone else who takes an animal early in the season when it's still warm should gut the animal out as soon as possible. If you shoot the animal and can't find him that day the odds are your meat has been spoiled by the next day. This is why I always give the animal plenty of time to "pile up" before I start tracking: at least one hour, unless I see him or hear him "pile up". If I track him a short distance and don't see a good blood trail I back off and return two hours later. Patience! This is especially important early in the season when there's no snow and everything is dry. The last thing you want is the animal to get up and run away with a poor blood trail. Adrenaline can make them run a good distance. Odds are you'll never find that animal again, especially if there is no snow for tracking.

There are multiple benefits to boning out your game in the field. When beginning the butchering process, I try to get the skin, glands and bone off the meat as soon as I can. Being a bow hunter and hunting often during 70 and 80° days, it is important to cool your game meat as quickly as you can. Many times when back in the bush, I have placed my game meat ON TOP of a creek to keep it cool, though try not to submerge your meat in the water too long because it won't last.

Once you have the animal down, gutted and skinned it's time to de-bone it. (Some people carry out the quarters with the bone but it's a lot heavier). When you are removing the meat from the bone try to remember to put it directly in your game bag in order to avoid getting it too dirty. To the seasoned hunter these suggestions might seem obvious, but there are likely some people reading this from urban America who have aspiration to hunt but don't know where to begin, just like I did when the 1974 movie "Jeremiah Johnson" came to the theaters. Then and there I wanted to come out to the northern Rockies and live my mountain man dream. The real "Jeremiah Johnson", by the way, was from New Jersey. Anything is possible! Read the book "Crow Killer", it is about this mountain-man.

After you remove the meat from the bone with your hunting knife, it's time to haul your game bags out of the woods. Now you're on the way home with your boned-out meat. You're filled with pride and achievement and you know you're bringing healthy game meat home with no steroids, hormones or antibiotics. From here it's up to you. Most people will cut up the meat, for example butterfly the back straps, wrap it up in freezer paper and stick it in the freezer. Some might put it through a meat grinder and wrap it up or can it. Some may just cut it up in small cubes and freeze it or can it. We obviously prefer to can everything because we don't own a freezer, plus, the shelf life benefits are much greater. Canned meats can last over 10 years where meat in a freezer can get freezer burned in as little as a year and a half. To me it's a no-brainer, especially when you're living off the grid and off the land.

It's also up to you which part of the meat you use for steaks, roasts, stew meat or burger. I like to steak the tenderloins, which are the strips along the lower spine. You can usually see them after you gut out your animal. Burger and stew meat will depend on your dietary preferences. I probably do a little more burger than stew meat because it is more versatile. For example; lasagna, chili, burgers, hamburger helper, meatloaf, meatballs etc. Nothing goes to waste around here. Some people prefer to smoke or jerky meat which I have also done on occasion.

Fishing

Wow, I've had a lot of excitement while fishing! I love to fish so much that I bought a piece of property with a small river running through it. I mostly fly fish but sometimes use a spinning rod, especially when the Kokanee salmon are running. In the winter, when ice fishing, I enjoy going to popular spots so I can use a hole another ice fisherman has already dug in the ice. Once in a while I have to drill my own ice fishing hole but, it's infrequent.

Having fished in many places across Montana I have to say that fly fishing on my own property has been the most rewarding. Living in the central western part of the state for 19 years has given me the opportunity to fish large rivers like the Clark Fork, the Bitterroot and the Blackfoot. I have also spent a lot of time fishing the legendary Rock Creek. During all this time on these great waters, I have caught a lot of fish. However, my biggest fish has come on my own property here in N.W. Montana: a 33 inch, 12 pound, monster bull trout caught on a fly rod. I have also landed a beautiful 26 inch rainbow trout and an 18 inch cutthroat trout. I can't tell you how rewarding it is to catch such big fish on your own land.

99% of the fish I catch I release. Don't get me wrong, I enjoy the taste of a good trout now on then, and salmon is the exception to the rule, especially when they are spawning up my river. If they are going to die after spawning, I'm okay with harvesting as many as the regulations allow. On the river we are allowed to keep 20 Kokanee salmon per day per person. On the lake where they spawn from, 50 per day is the daily limit.

It shouldn't matter if you fling the fly rod or use a spinner outfit. It's about the love of the outdoors. It's about the challenges and reaping glorious bounties from your efforts. Here in Montana, we probably have in the neighborhood of 40 different species of fish. I've caught just about everything that swims in this state including rainbow, bull, brook, cutthroat, brown trout and lake trout. I've caught mountain and lake whitefish, grayling, small and largemouth bass, burbot (ling), kokanee salmon, northern pike, sturgeon, paddlefish, catfish, sauger, walleye, crappie, drum, goldeneye, carp, sunfish and yellow perch. I know I've caught more but, this is all I can remember off the top of my head. I arrived in Montana at the age of 26, and if I had ONLY one goal: to fish all the waterways (including high mountain lakes) in Montana, I would still not be done. Montana is probably the most diversified state in the lower 48 for hunting and fishing. It would be up to you where to spend your time, depending on the species you would like to hunt and fish. Personally, I like to do it all because I like the variety.

It's Not Just About Survival – You Have To Love It

As I mentioned before, because of the health of my spine, my hunting options regarding locations has been greatly diminished. This is why I am very grateful for the following: First, getting to Montana at a young age. Second, having my little hobby farm and permission from good people (other land owners) who allow me to hunt their land. This of course gives me the ability to drive right up to my kill. Last year I had someone load my elk with a tractor. Then I had the butcher unload it from my truck whole with a winch. (The mountain men of the nineteenth century would be envious of the reduced work load.) I then donated the whole elk to a friend and that's why it ended up at the butchers. This worked out well since I was able to harvest a moose, later in the season.

I am also grateful for being given the foresight to see that our freedoms and liberties in this nation are deteriorating fast, especially for the middle class. I am grateful to experience what generations after me will be too afraid to do because it will be deemed "politically incorrect," be too expensive or just overregulated. I remember a news story from a while back in which they pointed out that today's kids, 13 to 26 years old, spend 64 hours per week on electronic toys. The saddest thing about it all is that these kids will be convinced by the "powers that be" that they are living a good life. In reality, our young people are dying of heart attacks, developing diabetes, suffering from gross obesity, and living day to day filled with anti-psychotic drugs and virtual reality. They will be very angry when they get into their 50's and realize that their adventure years have been wasted. I hope this book will change some young minds in urban/suburban America. I hope they realize that technology is manipulating everything from minds to financial markets.....it's killing America. Technology should be used as a tool and not a recreation, or at least 90% of the time.

I have always said that if I show you a child with a bow and arrow, hunting gun, or fishing pole in their hand, that will be one less adult on the street corner buying drugs or being depressed. Personally, I don't know how anyone can be depressed living in the country.

It's Really About the Outdoors

I don't want you to think that it is all about hunting and fishing. It's not just about the sport, or the survival knowledge; it's also about nature and appreciating it! In fact, if I had a time machine, I would go back to the year 1800 and sign up with the Lewis and Clark expedition. (Assuming I could be in my 20's again). That's how much I love nature!

For about two to three weeks in the spring when I'm fishing on my river, there is a scent in the air. As I'm casting my fly rod back and forth, I can smell the end of the service berry blossom mingled with the fragrance of the choke cherry blossom which is just starting. At the same time I can smell the beaver casters. This is the time when the adult beavers build a small dirt mound on the river bottoms while leaving their sent to attract mates and defend territories. Beaver casters, the glands by the base of the tail, are often the main ingredient used in colognes and perfumes. Just FYI.

Last year while "horn hunting" (I walk around the woods in late winter or early spring when the snow is gone or minimal and look for antlers that have been shed by deer, elk or Moose), I walked into a bedded down mountain lion on my property. He was only 20 yards away, our eyes connected, and I'm sure he said the same thing to himself as I did...... holy shit! I wish I had a camera! We looked at each other for about seven or 8 seconds each hoping that the one didn't see the other. After about 6 seconds, I pulled my knife out of my sheath, just in case he was going to attack, and to this day I will never know.... Did he run away at the ten second mark because he was frightened, or did he feel too vulnerable? My knife was only about 4 inches long and his five claws were probably that long individually, so, I could only assume that he ran away because he had to laugh real hard at my knife. If that mountain lion wanted to kill me, he could have done it with ease. I use my knife about five times per day and unfortunately, sharpen it only once a week. This particular day, I was out without my sidearm. Still, it was an awesome once-in-a-lifetime experience.

Another amazing experience I also had on my property during the last year was when I was salmon fishing on the river. I had been out for only about 40 minutes and had already caught my 20 salmon limit. I was on one knee in the river cleaning my fish when it happened. I was "false charged" by a bear. The brush was real thick at this part of the river bottom and I couldn't see more than 10 yards. I couldn't tell if it was a black bear or a grizzly. We do have our share of grizzly bears in this neck of the woods and I have seen quite a few in the wild. When he charged, he came within 15 yards of me and stopped. He was grunting and growling and the brush parted when he charged. I've been charged by bears before but never this close. When I was cleaning the salmon, I was right on the edge of a deeper hole in the river-about 8 feet. I had two plans of action if he attacked. Plan A was to show him my dull 4 inch knife blade and hope he would laugh himself to death, similar to the Mountain Lion episode. My plan B was to dive to the bottom of the deep hole in the river and hopefully avoid hand-to-hand combat.

Well, as you can imagine, I quickly decided that Plan B was the way to go. Thank God I didn't have to use either plan. I've told this story to a few people and, of course, I received a wide variety of advice to ponder. However, one piece of advice that was given to me came from someone who just moved here from the city and had just received his concealed carry permit. He said, "I wish I was there because I would have pulled out my 9mm pistol and shot that bear down."

OK, I'm laughing so hard right now that I accidentally started a new paragraph! First of all, never shoot a charging bear with a small caliber pistol. A 9mm isn't a bad gun to use for self defense for people but, for a charging bear, I would recommend a 44 mag. or at the very least a 357mag. "What if it's a grizzly bear" he asked? I told him if you're using a 9mm pistol you better file down the front site to be "flush" with the barrel. He said "isn't this going to compromise my aim?" I said "yep, but it won't hurt so much when that grizzly takes your pistol out of your own hand and shoves it up your ass".

I have had some incredible experiences in nature· from bears pawing at my tent at night; to me actually howling in a pack of wolves; stalking bears with a bow and arrow; sleeping on a hillside that was so steep I had to lay on a game trail so I wouldn't roll off the mountain; having a cow moose attack me because she was protecting her calf. I had to shoot at her feet twice to make her discontinue her charge. I can promise you one thing, a lot of these experiences make me sometimes forget my spine and arm pain for a brief moment. It could be calling in an elk to shoot with my bow or a rare bird I see on the riparian zone when fly fishing on my river-I will fondly remember these experiences for the rest of my life. I just hope that you, the reader, will get to feel similar kinds of adrenaline rushes in the outdoors and pursue a life in nature not only because you are concerned about our country deteriorating, but also because you love this exhilarating lifestyle of outdoor adventures.

I know every track in the woods from ungulate to fur bearer and I get so excited every time I see a new track in the snow or mud. I also have about two dozen cameras set up on my property which I highly recommend to everyone that owns a little bit of land. It's so much fun checking the pictures and seeing what you have caught on film. I have pictures of deer, wild turkey (we have lots of them here) elk, moose, coyotes, fox, mountain lions, bear, grouse, etc.

I am also careful to remember that things can get rough economically, politically and socially. Knowledge of hunting and trapping could be a lifesaver. One successful snare trap could mean the difference between survival and starvation.

Time and observation have taught me many things. For example, people who pine for nature also appreciate variety, new challenges, space, and tend to get bored very easily in the "cookie cutter" world. When I look back on my life I have realized that I have had different friends for different events because I needed that variety in my life. I had different friends at school (where I was really bored and day dreamed about being in the outdoors, especially in the fall). Nearly every different activity included different people to keep life more interesting. I realized that this was not a flaw but, a gift. Some of my activities included going to the gym, night clubs, pool halls, hunting and fishing, Boy Scouts, going to camp (day and overnight), playing football, baseball, hockey, motorcycle riding, chess, cards................I did it all because I needed that variety. The point I am making is, if you were born to enjoy variety and do not like being be bored with repetition, then nature may be calling your name too!

In fact, I can take this one step further! I think that all male hunters (especially archery hunters) in Montana should file for "Victim Group Status" during the months of September through January. This would give us an exemption from work, from being boy friends and husbands. We should get paid by the government during those months, at least until we reach the end of our adventure years (somewhere between 55 and 60.) It will be up to the discretion of each individual hunter.

I hope these accounts have kindled a spark for many readers and inspired you to get rid of the "blue light specials" in your life. I hope that you are able to set aside the silliness of the material consumption-obsessed world and discover something better. Perhaps you've decided that you want to hunt and fish because of our American tradition and heritage, because you want to be more self sufficient, or because you just want to eat healthier. You may want to feed your family meat free of hormones, steroids and antibiotics. It could be that you need more exercise and you can't go to a gym anymore. It could be that you just want to be out in nature to observe her beauty. Maybe you have a severe degenerative disease, as I do, and you need need a solution to help motivate some sort of physical activity. Remember, motion is lotion! No matter what your personal motivations, the important thing is that you break free from the drudgery of the cardboard urban/suburban life and reconnect. If you don't go out and use our fabulous renewable resources the "powers that be" will only make them available to the super wealthy. (Just what has happened in Europe.) Then this lifestyle will be over and the people living this way today will be considered the "Last of the Mohicans." As Americans, we must learn once again to provide for ourselves, whether it be food, recreation, exercise or a simple piece of mind.

Chapter 10: Gardening

The number one reason I garden is simply because I love it! Until you have gardened on your own, it is difficult to understand the excitement and satisfaction one gets from playing in the dirt. I don't look at gardening as a chore or a job but as a "recreational necessity." I only spend an average of 30 to 40 minutes per day gardening. It's just part of the variety-packed lifestyle I enjoy in Montana.

I have been gardening since I was a boy, but was forced to stop because the large number of old trees in my New York neighborhood created too much shade on my little garden plot. I also gardened when I was a pharmaceutical rep despite my travels. My garden wasn't much to brag about at that time but I did it anyway because of the delight it brought me and because the health benefits of gardening are obvious. Fresh, great tasting vegetables without pesticides and GMO's (genetically modified organisms) at your fingertips whenever you like; this is the dream of any person who understands the importance of good health.

There is enough readily available information derived from legitimate studies to suggest that GMO foods can cause cancer, organ failure, and even changes in our DNA. The "powers that be" have created a system of food production that eliminates all accountability, especially for big agrobusinesses like Monsanto. The producers of GMO foods are not even required by law to label them as GMO, which should be mandatory here in America. (There are so many countries around the world that do not even allow GMO foods.) Ninety percent of all soy products, for instance, are indeed genetically modified. So, when you go to the grocery store or a restaurant, you never know what you're putting into your body. For anyone who has kids, grand kids, or just wants to stay healthy, you must start thinking about your eating habits. Or, just produce your own food and remove most of the uncertainty

I usually grow about 25 to 30 species of vegetables and this includes tomatoes, cucumbers, two to three species of squash (winter and summer), corn, green beans, peppers, asparagus, rhubarb, peas, cabbage, broccoli, brussels sprouts, cauliflower, carrots, Swiss chard, chives, onions, garlic, horse radish, turnips, beets, several species of lettuce, spinach, eggplant, kale, parsley, parsnips, potatoes, radishes and lemon sorrel off the top of my head. I bet you didn't think that Montana could grow such a variety of crops, but with the right knowledge and effort, a fantastic garden can be grown almost anywhere. Anyone can master great gardening skills, through trial and error, in their own micro-climate. (It's easier here in the N.W. portion of the state because we have such low elevation, that's why this area is referred to as the "banana belt" of Montana). Some of these crops are rotated from season to season and I don't necessarily grow all of these every year. I also grow a few species of fruits as well. I have about a dozen or so apple, pear and plum trees, and I also grow some grapes, blueberries and strawberries.

In Montana, night time temperatures can be tough on the vegetables, but for root crops, it actually assists in creating strong root growth. This is why I use a technique called "organic, wide row-raised bed gardening". Raised bed gardening means exactly what it says. The bed or soil is raised up above the ground level. I like to have my raised beds at a minimum of 8 inches above the ground. I've use raised bed gardening in several ways: I have propped up the soil with boards (usually two inch by twelve inch lumber, then I use metal flashing on the inside to help keep the 2 x 12's from rotting too quickly).

Most of the time I use small logs harvested from my land and position them in a rectangle, put some soil in them, and voilà! A raised bed!

I have even seen people use raised beds with no peripheral or border support. It's up to you what you use, if anything, for your borders, but I do recommend raised bed gardening for every region and not just northern gardening zones. Raised beds will warm the temperature of the soil sooner in the spring and keep the soil warmer into the fall. This makes germination and root growth more productive. Raised bed gardening has multiple benefits beyond soil temperature. It also helps to retain moisture and nutrients, which leads to faster growing times and larger quantities of produce.

Here on my "hobby farm" I have nutrient poor glacial silt soil. So, containing nutrients within the raised beds is very important. I also place a heavy weed barrier, like newspaper or cardboard boxes (flattened), then lay a wire mesh on the bottom of the bed before I fill with soil. This might deter an ambitious gopher.

Vegetables get their nutrition from the soil. Raised beds keep the nutrition from leaching out too far from your plant roots. Many people fantasize about owning rich farming ground, but in reality, farm ground is highly overrated. So much of America's farm ground has been so mechanically, commercially, and chemically beat to crap (remember this descriptive word, we'll talk about it later), its productivity pales in comparison to smaller organic gardens! When you have farm ground that has been compromised by mechanical and chemical abuse, do you really want to feed those vegetables you do happen to eek out to your family? If the answer is no, then keep reading! I am also warning people often about the high levels of heavy metals in urban/suburban soil. Beware!

Let's say you have virgin ground, in other words, soil that has never been farmed. It's never been exposed to chemicals, gas, or oil (by the way, good luck finding that today). Having raised beds, instead of single row gardening, will still keep whatever vitamins and minerals you put into the soil trapped and ready for use. That's right; you are ultimately in control of what you put into your vegetables for consumption and that's a good feeling isn't it? Especially when eating raw vegetables as I often do. Another benefit in raising the bed is higher vegetable yields, less bending when weeding, easier picking and easier control of your perennial vegetables and fruits. For example, raised beds with borders keep my asparagus, sorrell, chives, horse radish, Egyptian onions, strawberries and raspberries from spreading too far beyond what I would like. Last, but not least, I don't need to use a rototiller. When doing raised bed gardening, as long as you don't walk on them too often, you don't need to use any mechanical tilling device. When I plant my vegetables, I merely use a pitchfork in the patch of dirt where I'm planting to loosen the soil. It's that simple!

Before we talk about seeds, I would like to discuss a little more about how I start and make my own soil. All of these raised beds, obviously, need soil. Every time I start a raised bed I buy a small load of local topsoil for each bed. I have a total of only seven outdoor raised beds and two small green houses (both of my green houses have raised beds). All of my raised beds combined constitute only about 1/10th of an acre. That's it! However, in that small space I can conservatively say that we can grow 90% of our own produce. We do shop for produce now and then, but usually at a farmers' market or the organic section of the supermarket. The rest is grown with our own hands.

Getting back to the soil. Remember that one word I told you I would get back to...that's right, crap! This word is actually its own category in gardening, though most people refer to it as compost. My home-grown compost consists mostly of goat, chicken and turkey droppings. A few times a year I will clean out the barn and the chicken coop to remove the old straw which is covered in excrement. I often call this "Brown Gold". I then transfer the brown gold to the compost spot. I rarely even turn the compost, I just water it a few times during the summer and by the second year it's cool enough to add to the garden. In fact, there are so many deer romping in the compost pile that I get extra droppings and crushed vegetation. Nothing on the hobby farm goes to waste. Every eggshell, radish top, banana peel, coffee ground, tomato stem, and everything else organic that most urban Americans throw away goes into the compost pile. Everything, and I mean everything around here gets used at least twice.

I would like to share some ideas of the benefits of an off-grid hobby farm and its recycling possibilities. Remember, off-grid living is also about frugality and sustainability of life.

All the empty feedbags, from dog food, cat food to chicken food, get recycled as garbage bags. Every piece of junk mail, paper towel, napkin, and cardboard box gets recycled as fire starter in the morning when lighting the wood stove. In the early winter, we move our goldfish from the garden pond and bring them inside the cabin. Once per week, we will take out the old water from the fish tank and replace it with fresh water. (We don't use a filter system in the fish tank because we are trying to cut down our electricity usage in the winter). That old water is re-used to flush the only indoor toilet we have. We know exactly how many amps of electricity we use for every appliance or luxury per day. I'm also proud to say that we only use about 200 gallons of water every 8 to 12 days. (I hope I mention this fact often). The exception is when watering the garden and the critters. For you "city slickers" out there, the term "critters", in this context, refers to our pets.

The concept of gardening for survival is very helpful in teaching us how too think in terms of reuse and avoiding waste where unnecessary. No one will function off-grid for long without efficient resource utilization.

Once you have your raised beds and fertile soil ready, you are doing well, but still not yet at the planting stage. We now have to build a greenhouse or two depending on your consumption of vegetables. I have two green houses that are on the small side. The first one was professionally built using polycarbonate siding attached to a simple stick frame. The second greenhouse is my homemade "jalopy". Believe it or not my homemade jalopy holds more vegetables and does a better job keeping out the frost than the "professional" greenhouse. Also, my homemade greenhouse only cost me a few hundred dollars while my professionally built greenhouse cost me $6000.

I built my homemade model using 2 x 6 boards for the ridge pole and PVC pipes for the sides. I found out, unfortunately, that PVC will eventually erode from the sun's rays, so, I added metal piping for the sides. I quickly discovered that the wind was putting a bow in my ridge pole. My girlfriend, Karen, came up with a great idea to use "cattle panels", which are 16 foot long metal panels with square holes. She had the idea to overlap the cattle panels over the ridge poles, connecting the top two thirds of each panel, using wire, to its mate on the other side of the wall of the greenhouse. So, in another words, it will look like an upside down "U". I then drove rebar into the ground and attached the cattle panels to the rebar. This turned out to be a great idea because of the stoutness of the panels. It has prevented more wind damage to my ridge poles and has created so much strength to my greenhouse that I don't have to worry about snow loads in the winter. Make sure you cover your greenhouse with UV treated plastic so it lasts.

Fencing, is also an important component of gardening and to keep wild animals out of your garden, otherwise you will lose an extensive portion of your crop to invaders. My property has numerous deer, unbelievable hordes of them! Along with a respectable number of elk and bear. Occasionally, a moose walks through my place too. So why do all the work to build your garden if you can't protect it from wild animals? I have used eight-foot wire square fencing in order to create a perimeter. You could also use a six foot fence and add a couple of strands of barbed wire on top. I prefer to use 10 foot metal fence posts, in lieu of wood, so I don't have to put in new posts every 15 years or so. This seems to do the trick, and our crop is always safe. At this point in my life, my arms sting and burn too badly so I don't pound the posts in myself. I just hire a teenager or some other worker to do these physical tasks.

Now you're ready to break out the seeds. People often purchase what they think will be the prettiest plants and do not think beyond that. This is a mistake. You want to make sure, first and foremost, that you buy and use heirloom seeds, also known as open pollinated seeds. These are seeds that not only grow great vegetables but they are also a pure variety that provide better quality, more nutrition, and their seeds can always be harvested for future generations. Regular store bought crops are unreliable at best, and often do not produce next generation seeds. Heirloom seeds are God's seeds. Standard store bought seeds are all to often laboratory seeds.

Here is a short list of some sources where you can get good, safe and healthy heirloom seeds/open pollinated seeds.

1) Seeds of change - www.seedsofchange.com
2) Baker Creek heirloom seeds - www.rareseeds.com
3) Native seeds search - www.nativeseeds.org

A word to the wise - always check and verify. By the time this book is on the market everything could change. Heirloom seeds could be very difficult to get and it's up to you to make sure they're not coming from an unethical company.

Do not, I repeat, do not buy seeds that are not "open pollinated/heirloom seeds". Do not buy seeds that are sold by Monsanto or any other chemical company. I personally don't recommend buying any seeds from a chemical company, especially, companies that do GMO research and distribution. Not to mention the fact that Monsanto has a reputation for suing farmers just because a seed has blown over, via mother nature, and pollinated on someone else's land. Today Monsanto, thanks to Congress, has protection from lawsuits.

Monsanto has been aggressively, but quietly, moving into the vegetable seed arena with the $1.4 billion purchase in 2005 of California based Seminis. This purchase gave Monsanto control over more than 30% of the North American vegetable seed market, as well as more than 20% of the world's tomato seed market and more than 30% of the global hot pepper market. You should be very concerned, especially if you have kids or grand kids!

Recently, Monsanto formed the International Seed Group Inc. (ISG) as a holding company for its growing investments in regional vegetable and fruit seed businesses. Unlike the Seminis business, which is primarily directed at the open field vegetable market, the bulk of Monsanto owned De Ruiter's business is for greenhouse growers. This is known as the "protected culture" market which Monsanto said is the fastest growing area of the vegetable seed industry today. Monsanto's vegetable seed business will now include De Ruiter seeds, the "protected culture" market, Seminis, the open field vegetable seed market, and the International Seed Group which will serve the regional seed business.

Monsanto is not the only chemical company buying up small seed companies. Syrgenta and Bayer are also buying up regional seed companies. In the corn seed business, it is hard to buy seed that is not owned by Monsanto, Syrgenta or Dow.

Here is a short list of seed companies owned by Monsanto:

-Territorial Seeds -Totally Tomato -Vermont Bean Seed Co. -Burpee -Cook's Garden -Johnny's Seeds -Earl May Seed -Gardens Alive -Lindenberg Seeds -Mountain Valley Seed -Park Seed -T&T Seeds -Tomato Growers Supply -Wilhite Seed Co. -Nichol's -Rupp -Osborne -Snow -Stokes -Jungs -R.H. Shumway -Seeds of the world -Seymour's Selected Seeds -HPS -Roots and Rhizome -McClure and Zimmerman quality Bulb Broker -Spring Hill Nurseries -Breck's Bulbs -Audubon

Workshop -Flower of the month club -Wayside Gardens -Park Bulbs -Park's Countryside Garden

I can expand on this list if I wanted to. Unfortunately, I also have a record of about 30 current varieties of seeds that Territorial admits purchasing from Monsanto/Seminis.

Remember all this information needs to be checked and verified prior to purchasing seed because it is changing everyday. The "powers that be" will do anything to hide GMO and any information from savvy consumers. Make sure your seeds are top notch, otherwise, all your garden work will be for nothing.

Now that your garden fences, green houses, and raised beds are completed, it's time to germinate some seeds. Before I open the door to the solarium, I warm up the potting soil in the cabin for a few days. I then take my potting soil and plant my seeds in small plastic containers that I used for germination. (Any nursery will have them in stock and there are many to choose from). I've used many different containers and they all work fine. I have even used soil blocks which will also work fine. Just make sure you have water drainage because seeds can rot very easy. I will leave my seeds to germinate on the kitchen table fairly close to the wood stove. Believe it or not, seeds prefer to germinate in warm temperatures with a little sun light versus cold temperatures even when there is lots of sun. A couple days after they germinate, I transfer the little plants to peat pots. I like peat pots because they disintegrate well in the ground and this helps to prevent root balling. (I also peel back the peat pots at least half way before I plant into the garden.) Root balling is when the roots grow so fast that they ball up and bind tightly to the sides of the container. This will stunt your plants growth and greatly reduce your vegetable yield. Cucumbers and some squash are notorious for this phenomenon.

After the vegetables have germinated I move them into the solarium. This is just a little glass frame extension that I heat with convection from my cabin. In other words, I just open the door that connects my cabin to the solarium and it heats it up. I usually open up the solarium for use sometime in late March. The days are plenty long and the solarium can heat up on its own from the sun. On cool days and nights, I leave the solarium door open to the cabin and the cabin heat will keep my little plants from getting frosted. It is so much fun to watch this first phase of the garden. Germination and early plant growth is so exciting because, just like the river that runs through my property, every day is different. Every day has new variety!

Different vegetables require different start-up or germination times. For example, I will start tomato and pepper seeds earlier in the season than I would cucumbers and squash. Peppers and especially tomatoes can be transplanted more easily. Tomatoes in my opinion even like being handled, where cucumbers definitely do not. I transplant a cucumber only once, germinating from a peat pot and then over to the greenhouse for final planting. I wait for my cucumbers and squash to have three adult leaves before I transplant them into my greenhouse. They won't have time to get root-bound and they will have a strong root base by this time. This means I will start my cucumbers later than the rest of my veggies. The cabbage family seeds, which includes broccoli, cauliflower, brussel sprouts, and obviously cabbage, will be planted as late as the middle of April. It's up to you to experiment on what works for you and your climate. The experimentation with seeds is so much fun, so don't miss out by buying too many pre-grown plants. On occasion, I will buy a few plants to fill in some holes in my garden but, the great majority of my vegetables are plants that I have germinated from seed.

One of my favorite garden vegetables is probably what most people would agree to growing – tomatoes. They produce fabulous tasting, beautiful fruits. These plants get up to 7 feet high and they will bear fruit until a hard frost kills them in the fall. In my neck of the woods, I've had my tomatoes go into late October and sometimes early November. November is rare but it has happened.

Don't forget to transplant small tomato plants up to three or four times before you plant them in your garden. Plant them as deep as you can each time so that their roots are strong and stems are thick. My favorite variety of tomato is called "Brandy Wine". The fruit can get double the size of my fist and has the best taste of any tomato in the world. This is an heirloom variety that has not been tampered with by a chemical company, just nature's God.

By early April, I start to transplant other small plants into bigger pots. By the third week of April I will diligently move my little plants outside to "harden" them for their big garden debut the first week of May. I can't stress how important it is to harden your plants for at least 10 days, (hardening means bringing your young plants outside in the morning and inside in the evening) you're doing a lot of work so why not do it right otherwise, your plants will probably die during the first couple of days in your garden. I even recommend covering your plants, depending on the species, when you first put them out in the garden. Don't forget to use UV treated plastic. I have even covered my young plants, at night, with old sheets or buckets. Just remember to uncover them after the sun is up and the frost has melted.

By mid April I am also planting a few things in the garden directly; this includes lettuces, Swiss chard, peas, and my root crops such as potatoes, turnips, radishes, beets and carrots. I often use some of the potatoes left over from last year as seed. I use the same philosophy with my spinach as well. I let some of the spinach plants go to seed and, in late fall, shake them over some of the raised beds and let them germinate on their own. It never fails; by early to mid March spinach has germinated in the garden. Do you know that if you let a second year carrot go to seed it will voluntarily reseed your garden plot? Don't forget to use heirloom seeds. As you can see, I spread out the plantings over a period of about a month so I don't have to kill myself doing everything at once. If you plan it right, it's a recreation and not a chore!

During the first to second week of May, I plant my greenhouses. This includes the tomatoes, peppers, squashes, beans, corn, cucumbers and everything else that is not cold hardy. I don't grow corn very often because, even though it tastes good, corn is not the most noted vegetable for nutrition. (It has OK protein though). Not to mention the fact that it depletes a lot of nutrition and water from the soil. Some folks around here don't use a greenhouse for these vegetables but my yields are usually 3 to 4 times higher, so it just seems like a no brainer to me! I also keep grapes, blueberries and strawberries in my greenhouse. Just remember, if you grow these plants in a greenhouse you need to water them at least once a month in the winter to keep the roots from drying. Even though it's winter with freezing temperatures this is a must! In the winter I will even dump some snow on these plants for moisture. In this portion of Northwest Montana, we get quite a few winter thaws and a surprising amount of rain, so the snow you put on your greenhouse plants will eventually melt.

In my greenhouse I also keep some mint family plants, specifically cat nip. The reason why I chose the catnip plant is because it blooms from early April into November. This plant helps attract bees and other pollinators into the greenhouse. Early in the season, I will also use a tiny little paintbrush and walk along the borders of the greenhouse raised beds and pollinate each vegetable flower myself. It only takes about 10 minutes per day and I only do it for the first couple of weeks until the pollinators have discovered that the plants are in the greenhouse.

By the end of the second week of May, I have everything planted in the garden (inside and outside of the greenhouse). For weeks now I have been harvesting spinach, lemon sorrel and chives for salads. We are now just a few days away from harvesting radishes and peas and I'm already harvesting asparagus. Soon after that I will have broccoli coming out of my ears! Tomatoes and broccoli are probably my favorite vegetables to eat.

By June everything is growing like crazy! The vegetables are getting large and are starting to cover the weeds. Because I use what I call "French style raised beds" there is some competition between plants. As the summer goes on I have less of a weed problem because the vegetables dominate the beds. I also try to mix up the vegetable species in the beds so there is less competition for the same vitamins and minerals. You just need to make sure that whatever vegetables you put together are compatible and are not competitive with one another.

Different species of vegetables require different amounts of watering. My favorite example is tomato versus corn, since so many people like to grow both. Tomatoes prefer it much dryer and are easy to over-water, while corn enjoys a lot of moisture.

I prefer to hand water, with a wand from the garden hose. This gives me an opportunity to look at every individual plant for insects and pests. It also gives me an opportunity to pull the occasional weed. You want to pull the weeds while the soil is wet anyway or else you will leave too many roots in the soil and you're basically just giving your weed a haircut. I prefer to not use a sprinkler system because it wastes too much water and waters too many weeds. I try to water only the vegetables and flowers. My girlfriend enjoys gardening with the flowers and I do the vegetables. It works out very well.

The next step is to focus on natural pest controllers that you can add to your garden. Marigolds, nasturtiums and mint are great flowers to keep away certain pests. Northwest Montana doesn't have a big insect problem for vegetable plants. The biggest issues I've had over the years are with the cabbage butterfly which produces the green cabbage caterpillar. And some slugs can be a problem for the cabbage family plants, which again includes broccoli, cauliflower, brussels sprouts and cabbage. There are four things I have found that work very well to deter these pests. The first thing is a product called "mosquito barrier". This trick was given to me by a commercial cabbage farmer up in British Colombia. This is a food grade, non-poison product which is 99% garlic juice. Secondly, I have also used sour milk with some success. The third trick is putting wood stove ash around each individual plant. This works great for slugs because they don't like crossing this rough gritty barrier. Plus, this adds extra nutrients to my soil. But, beware because too much wood ash can change you soil PH. And lastly, beer. The slugs will go into the beer and drown. Personally, I hate to waste good beer like that! During hot summers I use less pest controllers because the local wasps track down and hunt my caterpillars and slugs.

My next biggest insect foe is the spider mite. Mites are very, very small relatives of the spider, and some species feed on the sap of vegetables and flowers. Plants infested with mites often have a pale colored leaf or foliage covered with yellowish specks. Mites are most often found on the underside of leaves clinging to soft young stems, leaves and buds. My mite problem only occurs in the solarium and the green houses. The best way I've found to prevent mites is to make sure I open up both of my green houses all the way to the outside. For some reason mites prefer a closed environment. If that doesn't work, there are a plethora of organic sprays on the market. One product I use is called "All Seasons Spray Oil". I spray this organic product in my solarium and greenhouses a couple of days before I start planting. This oil will kill insects by smothering and prevent a successful egg hatch. This air circulation is why it's important to put up a greenhouse that has extra-large doors or at least a skirting that can be raised and lowered every day. Plus try and build your greenhouses long length to the wind direction, this will also help pollinate your flowers.

I don't test the pH of my soil. I know there are many serious gardeners who do but, I feel that since I supplement my soil with so much organic matter my garden should be fine. So far it's worked for me and I have used the same area now for 8 years. I try to rotate the vegetables every year so I don't deplete specific vitamins and minerals from one spot. I try and use only organic matter in my garden and supplement the raised beds with only a few things.

In addition to the compost, I use two organic products: One is called 8-5-5 and is an all natural and organic fertilizer containing nitrogen, phosphate, potash, calcium and less than 1% sulfur. The second product is glacial rock dust. This contains calcium, magnesium, cobalt, iron, manganese and sodium. As you can see, the common ingredient here is calcium. Calcium is very important to a garden and without calcium, you can get what's called 'blossom end rot'. I'm sure if you're a gardener you have seen these on your tomato, pepper and squash plants. It's very common on tomato plants. Blossom end rot can also occur from long periods of wet weather or over watering (It is very easy to over water a tomato plant). About once a year, during the winter months, I will sprinkle a little wood ash in the garden. Wood ash has Lime which can help add some calcium and increase your pH.

I concentrate on planting and consuming vegetables that are immune stimulants. These vegetables can fight cancers, tumors, and basically give your body the homeostasis it needs to survive and thrive. Some of these vegetables include broccoli, cabbage, brussels sprouts and asparagus.

My girlfriend also makes an organic tincture that we put on certain foods to "spice them up". It consists of garlic, onions, cayenne pepper, ginger root and horseradish. We grow the garlic, onions, peppers and horseradish. We buy the ginger root. She chops and blends everything up and puts them in some apple cider vinegar for preservation of shelf life. When we are in the mood to put it on our food it's like getting a shot of adrenaline. You can feel your immune system being boosted almost immediately.

I will include some books on gardening and food preservation to get you started.

Books for gardening in colder climates:
Four Season Harvest by Eliot Coleman
The Vegetable Gardener's Bible by Edward C. Smith
Seed Sowing and Saving by Carole B.Turner
Seeds of Deception by Jeffrey M. Smith

Food preservation:
Ball Blue Book of Canning
Country Living by Carla Emery
Home Cheese Making by Ricki Carroll
Growing and Canning your Own Food by Jackie Clay
Home Sausage Making – Storey books
Mary Janes Idea- Cook Book -Life Book by Mary Jane Butters
Home Food Dehydrating by Jane Shirley Bills
Cheaper and Better, Homemade alternatives to Store bought Goods by Nancy Birnes

Of course there are many, many more books and DVDs to get you started and even send you on your way to becoming an expert. I think that I will never be an expert for the following reason: When you consider yourself an "expert", you often stop trying to learn. Things can get old, the variety and excitement starts waning. I like and need variety in my life. This is my main reason for coming to Montana-to enjoy the four seasons to their fullest. All of my interests and hobbies overlap with seasonality and there are never any dull moments in nature. Gardening is an ongoing process of renewal, not just for the plants, but for you as well.

I would like to add a few names of food brands that is now owned by Monsanto. We heard this on "The Power Hour" in June of this year, 2013.

Aunt Jemima, Banquet, Betty Crocker, Bisquick, Cadbury, Campbell, Capri Sun, Carnation, Chef boyardee, Coca-cola, Duncan Heinz, Famous Amos, Frito-lay, General Mills, Green Giant, Healthy Choice, Heinz, Helmans, Hersheys-Nestle, KC Masterpiece, Kelloggs, Kid Cuisine, Koolaid, Kraft, Phillip Morris, Lean Cuisine, Lipton, Marie Callender's, Morning Star, Mrs. Butterworth, Nature Valley, Ocean Spray, Orville Redenbacher, Pepsi, Pepperage Farms, Post Cereals, Pillsbury, Prego-pastas, Pringles, Quakers.

By the way, one of the newest name for MSG is now E621. Are you ready to start gardening now?

Chapter 11: Health/immune system

First, I just want to say that if you don't think health care in America is politically driven, then I have another bridge to sell you. The bulk of Americans are losing their choices for health care, especially the middle class. Maintaining and improving your immune system, eating a healthy, nutritious diet and exercise will all help keep you healthy. Today, more than ever your health care will be up to you!

The "powers that be" are controlling every aspect of life in our so-called "free country". They control big Pharma, big agriculture, big chemical, Wall Street, banks and most financial institutions. So, because of this excess stress on the middle-class, I just want to share some think outside the box ideas to fighting cancer. Years ago you hardly ever heard of cancer. In 1900, one out of 60 people died of cancer. Today, 50% of Americans are dying of cancer.................. including children whose mortality rates are way too unacceptable. To simplify, cancer is a disease that exists because of a lack of good nutrition, hydration, exercise, sleep and we are being poisoned by an excess of exposure to chemicals in our food, water and air. Cancer is a multiple, variable deficiency disease. Unfortunately, we are all at risk of dying from cancer but, maybe if we all had more information, and acted on it, we could live longer and prevent this deadly disease from happening in some cases.

There are numerous enzymes in the body that are responsible for hundreds of chemical reactions which must take place to keep our bodies functioning normally. If our defense mechanisms are functioning normally, they will kill cancer cells and we won't even be aware it has happened. Cancer is a combination of many malfunctions of normal mechanisms in the body. These malfunctions are a result of a deficiency of chemical substances found in certain foods and of a deficiency of certain enzymes produced in the pancreas. Our pancreas is an extremely important organ. When pancreatic cancer occurs, survival rates are extremely low and usually results in a quick death.

A proper nutritional program should have two objectives. First, to provide the body proper nutritional ingredients in order to allow immunological defense mechanisms to function normally. Secondly, to take away from the body those things that are detrimental to its normal functions of its immunological defense mechanisms. Food is a fuel for the body like gas is for a car. If you don't give your car proper gas, it won't run correctly. If the fuel is old or has water in it, you won't get far!

Enzymes and vitamins are essential for healthy living. If you cook with temperatures over 130°F you destroy the enzymes which are important to fighting off cancer cells. All of us, especially during the winter months, eat a lot of processed foods. This includes frozen, canned, blanched, pasteurized and sterilized products. I recommend taking the summer months to enjoy fresh raw produce high in vitamins and enzymes. Look at it as a body cleansing to release toxins.

There are many tools on the market for fighting cancer, and by tools, I mean alternative therapies that are not chemotherapy, radiation or surgery. I can probably write a book on nutrition alone but, I'm trying to make as many purposeful, helpful messages in this book as possible. My motivations here are many. First of all, efficacy and survival rates regarding chemotherapy and radiation are statistically very minimal. I see so many people spending their life savings and dying a horrific death. My father was one of these people, and I wish I knew then what I know now. My Dad ended up with bone cancer and it wasn't fun to watch.

My first advice is to drink a lot of clean, clear, uncontaminated water. Not city water. I even recommend trying to stay away from most bottled water. Bottled water is laced with chemicals like chlorine and is often just tap water from some place else. I recommend water from a well that is at least 250 feet deep and is far away from other contaminants. I also recommend drinking half your body weight in ounces each day. For example, I'm in the neighborhood of 200 pounds. So, I try and drink 100 ounces of water per day. I also recommend eating foods that stimulate your immune system. I will go into some details and examples of which foods stimulate your immune system in edible plants and gardening chapters. For the most part they are vegetables and fruits that are fresh and free of pesticides.

I decided about two years ago, because of some symptoms I was having, to get some diagnostic tests. One of these tests was a CAT scan. Long story short, I had enlarged lymph nodes. I didn't tell anybody because I didn't want to cause worry. After doing a lot of research, I began harvesting "tea" from the forest. I harvested the tea from plant life that would stimulate my immune system. I ingested my tea for a good eight months or so before I had a second CAT scan and this showed that my lymph nodes were normal. I didn't get any of these lymph nodes biopsied, so I couldn't say absolutely that I had cancer, but, I can say without any doubt that these plants that I harvested made me healthier and increased my immune system.

Most of the pharmaceutical drugs that you're paying for are synthesized from chemicals and solvents, and are used along with many other molecules which are not healthy for the human body.

One book I highly recommend is titled "KNOCKOUT". This is a book written and researched by Suzanne Somers. She looks like she practices what she preaches (she looks 20 years younger than she is). Her book talks about the inadequacy of most doctors curing cancer, and how to prevent getting cancer in the first place. It talks about everything from nutrition to physicians you can contact in fighting this deadly disease. In case you are unaware, pharmaceutical companies financially support medical schools and the AMA; doctors are taught to dispense these drugs with no questions asked and give little if any nutritional information.

I'll be the first to admit there are some good physicians out there. Just like there are some good attorneys, I think. If an attorney calls himself a constitutional attorney, odds are his heart and mind are in a good place, just as some physicians have good hearts. But, one thing most of them don't have is the guts to research alternative therapies. They are afraid of going against the establishment, proven profits, and government kickbacks. There is a reason why the government requires an FDA approval on everything. Besides, they are also protecting the status quo. Unfortunately, it's mostly about the money.

For example, years ago physicians used to be able to hammer a plaque on their homes advertising their M.D. on the front door. Today, that's almost impossible. Most physicians can't exist without hospital privileges and the big attorney contracts backing them up. "Liability paranoia" has become overwhelming. So, when you look at the modern health system honestly, all you find is a massive controlled oligarchy. Hospitals, physicians, insurance companies and pharmaceutical companies control all protocol, regulations, and profits. In other words, the institutions of health, business, and government are in bed together. Just take a look at HIPPA regulations! They claim it's all about patient confidentiality, yet it has nothing to do with that! HIPPA was created to protect the establishment and hide the inadequacies of the mainstream system. Less leaked information about malpractice and swindling patients, less accountability for the establishment.

Don't get me wrong, there are some marvels within our modern health structure. America's physicians are excellent at many surgeries and traumas. But as far as nutrition goes, I would rather get my information from Nutritionists, Herbalists and Naturopathic Doctors. There are dozens of great books and loads of free information out there on the web. Mainstream doctors know little to nothing on the subject of nutrition.

Don't just depend on one web site, though; verify everything through multiple sites.

A quick word about surgeries. Some are unnecessary and even failures. I spent a few years as a patient at a "spine and pain" clinic in Kalispell, Mt. (thanks to GSK and political correctness) and saw too many failed back surgeries in the waiting room. This was confirmed by a physician, too. Plus they put me on a drug, for nerve damage, which was so debilitating I felt it was unethical to drive. I eventually took myself off of these daily-use drugs because they decreased my ability to think or even to speak clearly.

The web can have ambiguous information at times and it is up to you, the American consumer, to do your own research and make your own choices. If you are diligent in your analysis, you'll learn much; You'll uncover and discover a whole new world of nutrition and you may someday be compelled to move out to the country and supplement your own diet and medicines with wholesome natural cures. You'll also want to help your friends and family do the same thing. There are quite a few physicians curing cancers in the world, and outfits like the FDA are doing everything in their power to "silence" them. It's analogous to the central banks keeping the middle class around the world enslaved. I will share one example that will prove my point. This example should make everyone in the country and the world very angry. By the way, this is published information, but unfortunately most people are not aware of this example.

Stanislaw Burzynski, M.D., PhD. is a physician and a biochemist who has been treated unethically by the FDA and the National Cancer Institute. The "powers that be" take our taxes and spend between $5 and $10 billion per year on cancer research. I will try to shorten the story by many pages but, I will still prove my point.

Dr. Burzynski found a compound called anti-neo-plastons. Dr. Burzynski also discovered that there are some proteins and amino acids absent in the urine and blood of people with cancer. He also noticed that these proteins and amino acids were more present in healthy people. So, this man tried to help the people of the world. In 1977, he hired attorneys in his home State of Texas, to establish his own cancer research Institute. The attorneys and courts agreed that as long as he confines his research within the State of Texas, the federal government and the FDA has no jurisdiction. So, Dr. Burzynski started treating cancer patients with his anti-neo-plaston therapies. Patients with incurable cancers were going into remission quickly and without side effects. Patients from all over the world were coming to see Dr. Burzynski.

In the early 1980s, the FDA filed a civil action against Dr. Burzynski. The FDA even sent a threatening letter to a judge stating they would be forced to use "more severe and less efficient remedies" to stop him if the court failed to do so. The court did rule initially in Dr. Burzynski's favor and FDA attorneys were bragging that "they had other ways to get him." In the mid-80s the FDA publicized that Dr. Burzynski was under criminal investigation. Later that year, the FDA raided Dr. Burzynski's clinic and stole over 200,000 pages of research documents and patient records. Soon after, the FDA convened a grand jury in an attempt to bring an indictment against Dr. Burzynski. The grand jury found no wrong doing and would not permit the filing of any formal charges against him. Let's hope and pray, folks that we never lose jury trials because, if we do, your kids and grandkids will never be free. They will be told what to do, what to say, what not to say and how to think...............forever! Some folks feel that we are getting very close to that point already.

A year later the FDA conducted another raid on Dr. Burzynski's clinic. They stole another hundred thousand pages of research documents and patient records. Then convened another grand jury and again a finding of no wrongdoing. In 1986, the Texas State Board of Medical Examiners said that even though there weren't any complaints, they were starting an investigation and he should "lawyer up." The board even tried to convince him to stop his practice. Two years later they threatened to revoke his medical license. Two years after that the board filed an amended complaint with similar charges. Again, the Court could not find any wrongdoing and no action against his medical license was taken. In the same year, the FDA convened a third grand jury. More harassment but still no formal charges were filed. For the next two years the FDA continued to harass Dr. Burzynski. More complaints by "the powers that be" followed over the next couple of years and still no charges. 60 of Dr. Burzynski's patients petitioned against the Texas State Board of Medical Examiners to stop harassing him. Immediately the Board requested that the patients' petitions be stricken from the record.

Eventually the case went to trial and, after a fourth grand jury in 1994, the jury once again found no credible basis for formal charges. The FDA even subpoenaed all medical records of patients who had appeared on television praising Dr. Burzynski's treatments. The FDA convened a fifth grand jury in 1995. At no point did the FDA claim that Dr. Burzynski's cancer treatments were not safe or that they did not work. The only complaint was that the treatments were "unapproved". Within these restrictions the grand jury finally issued indictments for 75 counts of violating federal law and fraud. If convicted, Dr. Burzynski could receive 290 years in federal prison and fines of over $18 million. At the same time, the Texas State Board of Medical Examiners put Dr. Burzynski on a 10-year probation.

Because of pressure from the public, the FDA was forced to drop all but one of the remaining charges. Later that year Dr. Burzynski was acquitted on the final charge against him. This Nazi-like campaign cost the American people over $60 million and $2 million to Dr. Burzynski. The public, outraged, helped cover Dr. Burzynski's legal fees. All of this money would've benefited the entire world if it could be spent on furthering Dr. Burzynski's research instead of fighting these outlandish charges.

Unfortunately, this whole scenario gets worse. The National Cancer Institute, like the FDA, is part of the US Department of Health and Human Services. The National Cancer Institute had established an agreement with Dr. Burzynski to test his anti-neo-plaston therapies. As it turns out, they were using doses that were so small they were therapeutically non-efficacious. This was done intentionally to destroy Dr. Burzynski's credibility. You can see a documentary online............... if it hasn't been pulled. Part of the story is on www.burzynskimovie.com.

The fact is that chemotherapy drugs have generated trillions of dollars in revenue since their inception. In general, they do not cure cancer and have terrible side effects. Big Pharma, the FDA, and the National Cancer Institute are just trying to protect the status quo. In other words, their profits. I've read studies that show the NCI doesn't even care about survival rates. For example, if a tumor has gotten smaller from chemotherapy they call it a success, even if the patient dies. If the patient lives but the tumor doesn't get smaller, it goes into the books as a failure. In fact, in 38 states it is illegal to recommend any cancer therapy other than surgery, chemotherapy or radiation. Chemotherapy is basically a mustard gas developed back in the WW1 era.

I urge every American, and everyone around the world, to do your own research on alternative therapies that could possibly save a loved one or yourselves. You will learn so much. Facts like Tumeric being the best spice to fight and prevent cancer. Did you know that fatty fish like wild salmon can reduce your cancer risks? (Be careful, there is a lot of GMO/farmed salmon out there.) Do you know that Vitamin D 3 is the best single vitamin to fight and prevent cancer. Talk about these topics to everyone, learn from everyone, and share your information and live!

There are many of other alternate therapies that include nutrition, intravenous high-dose vitamin C therapy and dozens more that have cured cancer. Look into manganese, magnesium, selenium and vitamin B. Did you ever here about ESSIAC therapy? Look it up! Did you know that vitamin B-17 has helped a lot of people to fight cancer? There are books written about this one vitamin. Every author will tell you that vitamin B-17 is just one piece of the nutritional puzzle in fighting cancer.

I've also seen cancer charts researched from around the world. It should be very curious to everyone as to why so-called wealthier countries, which include North America, Western Europe, Australia and New Zealand to mention a few, have higher cancer rates than some of the poorest countries around the world. This includes countries with poor sanitation, whose people often suffer from diseases like dysentery. Could it be that the citizens of richer countries take too many drugs, like vaccines, to "prevent" other diseases? Are compounds like Mercury, fluoride and others that are being injected in our children creating cancers? How come 1 out of 100 babies are born with some form of autism or down-syndrome? Unfortunately, too much evidence is showing up to refute these so-called "good faith" prophylaxis drugs. Corruption and money all to often run parallel like rails on a train track. I'm a firm believer in physical exercise, (even if it's just walking), a good healthy diet of foods that stimulate the immune system, lots of hydration, and eliminating as many chemicals from your daily life as possible. I think most people by now know that sugar feeds cancer. In other words, it's an immune suppressant.

Some chemicals like MSG, aspartame and other artificial sweetners, nicotine, high fructose corn syrup and many more are designed to be addictive. Propylene glycol is an additive in many foods-did you know that this product is used for keeping pipes from freezing?

There are too many "food-like" products on the market today. "Fat free" usually means high sugar content that then causes the pancreas to produce excess insulin. Breads and carbs turn into sugar, which makes you fat if you can't burn off those calories. To put it bluntly America is over-fed, undernourished and under-exercised.

Did you know that American's have spent billions of dollars on fad diets and pills? What a waste of time and money! These are phoney industries just taking you're hard earned money. If you want to lose weight, buy a juicing machine. Buy organic vegetables and juice them. If you did this, ONLY, for three months while exercising you will lose a ton of weight, prevent cancer, and get much more nutrition than you're getting now. Do your research on juicing techniques and exercise, there is a lot of information on the web. Don't risk your life by getting your stomach stapled, it's the addictive chemicals and lack of nutrition that is killing us.

Always look at who "funds" the studies. For example, the pharmaceutical companies fund their own studies. Did you really think the FDA funded these studies? Hello! The FDA just publish what they've been given.

Try to remember my own personal acronym. SARP- this means trying to avoid anything Synthetic, Artificial, Refined and Processed. I know it's impossible to be perfect but try to reduce the intake of these four things as often as you can. I'm the first to admit that I have a sweet tooth! I love ice cream and desserts and I even eat pizza at least once a month. I try to eat all the "bad stuff" in moderation. We don't have to be perfect, just try a little harder.

I hope this nutrition/cancer information will help motivate some people to do more homework regarding thinking outside the box since this deadly disease is killing 50% of Americans; that is one out of two people! Who's standing beside you right now? Will cancer claim you or them?

Despite all the progress we have made by removing tumors with surgery and diagnosing cancer earlier, there has been no increase in survival time for cancer victims for over 50 years. Most of the rhetoric is about politics and propaganda. In other words, we are treating the symptoms (like the tumor) and are doing absolutely nothing to prevent the spread of cancer.

We need to have our own defense mechanisms functioning normally. Good nutrition heals and boosts the defense mechanism and not the body's tumor.

There is plenty of "hidden information" out there in the medical world. Unfortunately, unless it's something practically incurable like pancreatic cancer, the "good" information only goes to the "right" people.

Let's take another disease like AIDS. This disease kills similarly to cancer since it attacks a patient's immune system. Just asking, why has Magic Johnson lived so long with AIDS? How many thousands of people have died from AIDS since his diagnosis? Is it because he's a sports hero and has lots of money? Just asking! Even disease research has politically correct "undertones". In other words, some diseases get more legitimate research than others, while other diseases like cancer research have been dubbed a cash cow money-maker for the pharmaceutical companies and the "research organizations".

These days, we as a culture have abdicated our responsibility to contribute to the future. From health, to finance, and beyond, we as Americans have to start educating each other, and stop waiting around for corporations and government entities to do it for us. We have to take matters into our own hands, and change the system to our benefit, whether it is politically correct or not. This work begins not with charities, social welfare organizations, or "official" authorities; it begins with you and me as a free thinking individuals. Your willingness to help others in any way can encourage the same in those around you, and can indeed trigger a tidal wave of independent action. We can no longer rely on the state to fix all our problems. The state is broken, and a broken system is incapable of mending the ailments of others. It is time for us to step in and take over.

I bet there are many of you that thought "why is he writing about health and cancer fighting tips" in a book that is supposed to be about the financial, economic, social and political reasons for being self-sufficient? Well, if you need to be coaxed into making your family healthier, less obese, living a higher quality of life and reducing the risk of dying earlier in life, then no one can help you! This chapter should be your last wake up call, especially since health care has become so political. Trust me it will continue to become more corrupt and more rationed.

Here are a few extra health resources: Most can be found on line from Amazon or ebay.

Natural Remedies Encyclopedia, 5th addition by Vance Ferrell, Harold M. Churne, M.D.

Prescription for Nutritional Healing by James F. Balch, M.D. and Phyllis a Balch, CNC.

Where There Is No Doctor by David Werner

Where There Is No dentist by Murray Dickson

Bacterial Warfare, a Major Threat to North America by Larry Wayne Harris

Do-it-Yourself Medicine by Ragnar Benson

Survivalists Medicine Chest by Ragnar Benson

The Prepared Family Guide to Uncommon Diseases by Enola Gay with Maurice Masar, M.D.

The Safe Shopper's Bible by Steinman and Epstien, M.D.

Nurishing Traditions by Sally Fallon

Cancer: Step Outside the Box by Ty Bollinger

Some DVD's:
Blue Gold
King Corn
The Future of food
The Gerson Miracle
Burzynski, Cancer is serious business
The Beautiful Truth
The World According to Monsanto

There are so many good books and information available on any topic from anatomy to nutrition. I highly recommend doing your own research because today's physician has been indoctrinated by the pharmaceutical industry to prescribe synthetic drugs that have a list of side effects and contraindications as long as the trunk of an elephant and Pinocchio's nose combined. (Yes, that last analogy was a metaphor.) Most physicians are not trained for more than three or four semesters in nutrition. Proper nutrition is the best prophylactic treatment for most diseases and chronic disorders. But, beware of the Nutrionists hired by the "establishment". For example, if they say that GMO foods are safe or to keep ingesting chemicals..........run!

Chapter 12: Hobby Farm Animals

Though often portrayed in mainstream television and film as endless work and misery, having farm animals is actually a very relaxing and fulfilling hobby. Everyday I wake up to the sound of a rooster crow and a turkey gobble and it gives me so much joy. While it is true that our livestock must be cared for on a daily basis, we look at it as a privilege and not a chore. If we go anywhere for more than a day, we always have a house sitter, because I feel it is unethical to leave these beautiful animals unattended. They require care and attention, and if one is willing to take the extra responsibility, he or she will be greatly rewarded.

Having animals will also give you an excuse to go outside (not that I need one because I practically live outside). Other benefits include exercising the body and mind. When I see all my animals walking by each other with such synergy it makes me feel good. They all have different roles and accept them with a great pride. My chickens walk 6 inches away from the nose of one of my dogs, yet the animals all work together, and I work with them to make my off-grid farm more sustainable. I believe the American people could learn a lot if they all began raising some farm animals. It's a barter exchange between the animals and myself; we have consummated a deal. I have the pleasure of giving them food, water and shelter, and they pay me back with natural resources and services. The dogs guard, the chickens and turkeys supply eggs and meat, the goats supply milk for cheese and the entertainment value is never-ending.

Every beginner in off-grid living wants to know the simplest, most cost-effective and functional animals for their hobby farm, but this preparation depends on your needs, wants and desires. The first animal every hobby farmer should invest in is chickens. I've wanted to raise chickens since I was a boy back in New York, and the benefits of these creatures are obvious. By spring time, we get a respectable amount of eggs per day, and egg production remains steady as long as they are given a warm coop and a safe environment. In the wintertime we get very few eggs because the chickens are not getting enough light. Because I live "off grid" and make my own electricity, I make certain sacrifices in the winter. I try and be very frugal with electricity use and that is why we don't keep a light in the hen house. If you want to increase your egg production in the winter, simply install a light.

We occasionally eat a few chickens during the course of the winter depending on how many peeps/chicks we get from our chicken flock during the previous summer. We harvest the extra roosters and older hens for eating during the winter months. This saves us a few dollars because we don't have to feed the bulk of our flock all winter. We try to end up with about 5 chickens and one rooster by the time winter is over. I don't recommend having more than two roosters per 10 chickens because the roosters will fight and one of them will most likely die. We usually keep about two or three turkeys (only one Tom) as well.

And, of course, don't forget about the third benefit of having chickens..."brown gold". Nothing goes to waste here on my hobby farm and that includes the chicken poop. All that straw laced with "brown gold" goes into my compost pile to supply nitrogen and other nutrients to my garden.

I use an old, twelve foot 1960's trailer as my chicken coop. It's kind of a Taj Mahal for chickens but it has a lot of functionality. I can keep quite a bit of chicken paraphernalia in their coop. This includes everything from watering containers, chicken feed, rubber bands for identification, straw, peep feeders, nesting boxes and anything else that might come in handy. The first thing you need to decide is what kind of a chicken coop you would like to build or buy. Your style will be influenced by your climate, size of the flock, local predators, and your wallet. I like to have a high fence around my chicken coop area and occasionally I will put some bird netting over the top as well. This will help keep hawks, ravens, and other flying predators away from your flock.

Because I live on a river, I also get my fair share of bald eagles, ospreys and owls. At night most people have to close the door to their chicken coop and open it again in the morning. I will tell you later in this chapter why I don't have to do that. I also have a couple of exit/entrance holes so my chickens and turkeys can have free range. During the spring, summer and fall, they enjoy eating grasses, buds, seeds and especially insects. This really helps reduce the grasshopper population in the summer and early fall which directly helps my garden. This free range gives my birds the opportunity to dine on a variety of foods that make them healthier. If your birds are free range, you must make sure that neighborhood animals, like dogs, will not get near them. Most dogs will instinctively chase and even kill chickens.

There are many chicken breeds but I personally prefer the Buff Orpington variety. They are a reddish beige color and larger in size. I chose this variety for three reasons:

First, they have a reputation of being a good egg layer and brooder. Brooding means that they have the patience to sit on eggs and hatch them out into chicks. Last summer one of my "Buffs" successfully hatched 13 chicks. Secondly, they are also a good meat bird. This means they are a great bird to eat: good-sized and great tasting. Third, they do well in northern climates. I have two other species of chickens; Polish Crested hens and Silkie Bantam hens. These two breeds can have a tough time when the mercury dips below zero. It may only happen an average of 3 days per year here but they are not happy birds when it does.

I purchased a couple of Polish Crested hens because I thought they were cool looking. They have a huge tuft of feathers on the top of their heads that would make some peacocks jealous, but again, they are not as hardy in cold weather. Silkie Bantam hens look like little white snowballs and are entertaining to watch, but they actually have a purpose beyond being cute and tiny. They are fantastic brooders. If they have decided to start brooding with one of their own eggs, I will just place the eggs of other hens next to it. In 21 days...voilà baby chicks.

I love having baby chicks on the farm. It's just a lot of fun! They are so cute! If you want to produce a lot of baby chicks, however, I recommend getting an incubator. We are satisfied with producing between five and 15 babies per year because this maintains our flock size. If you only want a reasonable number of baby chicks per summer, then I would recommend breeds like the Buff Orpington's and Bantams because of their brooding qualities.

Another easy starter animal for the hobby farm are goats. I initially wanted goats for several reasons. My first desire was to use them as a 'pack animal'. Hunters and outdoorsmen alike are using pack goats for transporting their camp and gear into the woods and packing their harvested animal out. Just in case there are some people who never thought you could use a goat as a pack animal, there are indeed certain species of goats you can use. There are at least eight major breeds of goats recognized in North America. I consider only four species as large enough to be "pack goats." These species are the Saanen, Toggenburg, Alpine and Oberhasli. We have the Saanen goat. This goat is all white and is originally from the Saanen Valley in Switzerland. We also have one Sabel Saanen with the face coloring of the Sable antelope. The bucks, especially the "fixed" ones, are called "wethers", and can get up in weight to over 300 pounds and easily carry up to one quarter their weight. I can easily carry several goats in the back of my pick up truck at one time, and therefore don't need an expensive truck and trailer to do the hauling like one would need for horses.

I initially started looking into pack goats because I knew my health was deteriorating fast and I wanted to keep hunting, camping and hiking as long as I could. Remember, moderation and modification is one of my motto's. I've been lucky enough, though, to have other people pack me in and out of the woods. In addition to that, some private landowners have given me permission to hunt on their land so I can drive a vehicle close to the harvested animal, so using my goats for packing has not yet been necessary.

My girlfriend, Karen, has created a new hobby for herself as well. She loves to milk the goats and make homemade cheese. She can make seven kinds of goat cheese and I have to say that they are all tasty and top quality. She makes marscopone, chedder, swiss and mozzarella, most often. She milks about four months out of the year and sometimes as often as two times per day. Just from one little female goat she can get up to 1 gallon of milk per day. Now that's impressive! And this milk contains no chemicals or GMO ingredients. Saanen goats are really good milk goats but the best milk goat, by most people's standards, is the Nubian. I built a milking station for Karen to use, and the goats just jump on it by themselves with a little enticement of oats. The milking station is also used for inspecting the goats' health and trimming their hooves.

Another reason I wanted goats was for their grazing abilities. As most people know, goats will eat most vegetation. Unfortunately, that also includes your vegetables, flowers and fruit trees. This is why everything needs to be fenced. It's not really much extra work when you live in Northwest Montana because you have to protect all this vegetation from deer, elk, moose, and bear anyway.

Most goats are not too picky when it comes to eating grasses and even most weeds, making them ideal for reducing fire hazards and practically eliminating the need to mow your grass. And of course, there are fertilizer benefits as well. All the goat poop from the barn goes into the compost pile for future garden soil. Just like the chickens, everywhere the goats roam they fertilize my grasses. Everything on my hobby farm gets recycled, reused and works in synergy.

I have about 12 acres of fenced pasture that I use for three goats, on average. During the spring and early summer, we have a few more goats because of new babies. In winter, we usually keep two does and one buck. Twelve acres for goat pasture is just about right for them during the eight months of grazing here in our climate. This way I don't compromise the health of my grass. I only have to stock about a ton of hay for the four winter months. This is approximately 35 to 40 bales of hay, which is nothing compared to feeding a horse or a cow. By mid-March, 99% of the snow has melted off of my land, but that doesn't mean the grass is green and long enough for grazing. We usually start feeding the goats hay sometime in early December and continue through early April. The point here is that goats are very easy to keep, easy to feed, easy to breed, easy to milk and fun to watch. They make great pets and will often follow you around like a dog.

Baby goats are cute, acrobatic, and quite amusing. Every year, usually in April, we get between two and four baby goats and by mid-summer we give them away to a good home. When I say good home, I mean someone who's going to treat them like a pet and not eat them. Karen often laughs when I say that, but it's hard to give away a pet for someone's food when you have cuddled, petted and cared for the little critter. We have one rule: never name your food. It's just easier that way. So, I name all the goats.

I have raised several pigs specifically for food and they are also easy to keep. Because they are omnivores, they will eat just about anything! Pigs grow extremely fast and can put on two to three pounds of weight per day. Pigs are also very useful for breaking ground. During the pioneer days, the homesteaders would let pigs and goats out in their young forests and before you knew it, the land was pasture ready. I butcher my pigs when they reach about 250 pounds, and believe it or not, it takes only a few months for them to reach this size.

We have a couple of cats that live in the barn and they play a vital role. Just like most cats, these love to hunt and are excellent at it. If you have ever lived out in the country you know that there are mice everywhere. Mice and especially rats infest cities as well, but most people don't see them because they are nocturnal. Having a couple of cats has made a big difference in reducing the rodent population in and around my hobby farm. Cats eat very little and are exceptionally grateful for what they get. In fact, the cats here on the hobby farm have a great life. They go where they want, when they want, eat, and hunt and hunt and hunt and hunt. Sounds like a pretty great life to me!

Now, I did not have a pet until I was in my early 40's. The point of confessing this is to let you know that you can start a new life at any age. Granted, I was dreaming about this life since I was a teenager, but if your desires, interests, passions and dreams are going in a certain direction, then it's your obligation to follow them.

Last, and definitely not least, are the dogs… The dogs I keep on my hobby farm are called Great Pyrenees. This is a very beautiful dog that specializes in guarding, a job they have specialized in since the days of

Julius Caesar. I have three Great Pyrenees dogs guarding the other farm animals and they are irreplaceable! They are loyal, low keyed, but can be very ferocious when provoked by a predator, especially a human.

One afternoon we were playing in the garden and heard a commotion over by the chicken coop about 100 yards away. We had a line of sight to the coop, but this happened in a matter of seconds. After the commotion was over we approached the coop to see what had happened. Despite being mid-afternoon, a pack of coyotes sneaked in and took 11 chickens. This is when I started to look around for guard animals.

I looked at everything from llamas, to birds that give a warning call, to multiple species of dogs. For all of the traits and characteristics that I was looking for, my research kept leading me to the Great Pyrenees breed. I have three of them now running around in my goat pasture everyday. Since I have bought the dogs I have had zero problems with wild animals. This includes lions, coyotes and bears – oh my! I don't even have to close the door to the chicken coop because I know the dogs will keep them safe.

Additionally, I know of a lot of people who have large and even medium-sized dogs to protect their livestock from wild animals. A lot will depend on your hobby farm set up. The size of your pastures, topography variations? How close you live to your animals, do your animals have a barn to sleep in at night? There are many extenuating circumstances that could make you decide to find a guard animal. There are many different birds of prey here which usually don't mix well with free range poultry. I have seen my dogs stop an aerial attack from birds of prey many times. These dogs will keep all wild critters away. The river here attracts many wild animals and not just undulates. Potentially, I could have my chickens attacked by many other smaller animals such as fox, mink, otter, weasel, raccoon and more.

As far as Great Pyrenees, this breed of dog should be considered less of a pet and more of a working animal. These dogs need to have a job and it's unfair to keep them as indoor pets or trapped in a kennel or dog run. They are only happy when they are guarding outdoors. I have seen too many people buy this dog because they are pretty; and their looks should not be a consideration. They are lovable but are also workers. I have also seen many people and rightly so, complain about these dogs because they bark so much. Too many people buy these dogs for subdivision living; to me this is cruel to the dog and inconsiderate to the neighbors. This breed of dog has been bred to guard outside so it will bark often when on alert. These dogs have a great sense of smell and hearing so when they smell a lion, coyote, bear or another human, they are going to make a racket. I recommend anyone who has any barking dogs to be at least 100 yards from your nearest neighbor. It's just common consideration!

We also have a little 5 pound dog named "Killer". He is half miniature shelty collie and half toy poodle. He is the cutest and sweetest little animal I have ever met in my entire life!

I also don't want to ignore the entertainment benefits of farm animals, especially, in the spring. We get so much enjoyment out of babies running around the farm. It doesn't matter if it's chicken peeps, turkey pullets, puppies, kittens or baby goats...it's always a good laugh! Karen calls this phenomenon "Farm TV." I know it sure beats the hell out of watching regular television, which is filled with so much subliminal, politically correct ideology bull, I personally cannot understand how it can be considered recreation. To me it's just added stress and propaganda. Farm life is natural and real. No manipulations here. Just reality and the beauty of nature.

There are so many things I can write about regarding hobby farm animals. Some of these topics could include butchering, cattle, horses, sheep, rabbits and other farm animals, breeding, disease, medications, cheese making, game recipes, milking. There is just too much information to put into a book of this much variety. As with every chapter in this book, my main objective is to spark an interest and motivate, so you, the reader, can "take the ball and run with it". Remember, this is your hobby farm so it is up to you to choose which hobbies and interests you would like to pursue.

Here are a few good books on animal care to get you started...

Backwoods Home Magazine. This is one of the best "how to", self-sufficient magazines on the market.

The Pack Goat, by John Mionczynski

The Chicken Health Handbook, by Gail Damerow

Barnyard in your Backyard, edited by Gail Damerow

Natural Goat Care, by Pat Coleby

Keeping Livestock Healthy, by N. Bruce Haynes

Storey's guide to Raising Pigs by Kelly Klober

Veterinary Guide for Animal Owners by C.E. Spaulding, D.V.M. and Jackie Clay

Hoeggers Goat supply www.hoegerfarmyard.com

I use wood heating and prefer it ten to one over any other method. Wood heat is dry and warms up your bones, as opposed to propane heat which can create some humidity. I also like the fact that I can harvest my own heat source-wood. It's a nice feeling that I can use my chainsaw for only about 20 minutes per week and still get the nine chords of wood I need per year.

When I go harvesting wood I call it "woodhawking." This is a term used back in the early 1800's by the American mountain men who came Northwest to live. When these men weren't having success trapping they would resort to "woodhawking". These men would leave cut firewood piled on the Missouri River banks for the steamboats. In return, the riverboat captains would leave behind a small pouch of gold in a nearby hiding place-sometimes in the hole of a stump.

How many times have you entered someone's home who has conventional heat and froze your butt off? It happens often because conventional heat is expensive, especially electric and propane. One of the best attributes of a wood stove is temperature variations within your home. If you're too cold you snuggle closer to the stove or if you're like me (someone who prefers it cooler) you hang out closer to a window on the other side of your home. A home that has a wood stove can satisfy every person's temperature preference. There is no more need to fight over the thermostat setting.

I mostly use Douglas fir and Western larch for my firewood as these species of wood are the most common here in northwest Montana. I would say that 70 to 80% of my firewood is Fir and Larch. The other 20 to 30% is lodgepole pine, spruce, aspen, birch and ponderosa pine. Fir and larch have the best BTUs (this is British thermal units which means how much heat you're going to get from that particular piece of wood). I am a firm believer in spending a little time every week getting a few pieces of firewood and this way it never feels like a chore.

I use a wood cook stove in my cabin that is made by the Amish and is called the "Kitchen Queen"; it is also considered the "Cadillac" of wood cook stoves. The oven is the same size as a conventional oven and the fire box offers a very large opening for the biggest pieces of wood. Besides the obvious of heating a home, my woodstove gives us the ability to cook and heat water. In the summertime we use a "camping style" propane stove on the porch.

A wood stove has some peripheral benefits as well. For example, the wood ash has multiple uses. We use wood ash for supplementing our garden so we can add extra vitamins and minerals into our soil. Wood ash also comes in handy to sprinkle around your cabbage family plants. I sprinkle some of the ash around my plants to keep caterpillars and slugs down to a dull roar. I also use the wood ash for dumping into the outhouse. The lime in the ash helps disintegrate the waste while reducing the smell. Ash also gives us the benefit of creating traction on my frozen driveway; this is especially handy in February and early March when the ice is in the process of melting. During this time, the ice melts during the day and then freezes at night thus creating a slicker surface on my driveway.

Solar Power

I am a little unsure of how to pursue this topic in writing. The solar array scenario could intimidate some people. In fact, any mention of creating one's own power source can be kind of scary. That being said, the first thing I would like to say is that I started with absolutely no skills regarding alternative energy. None, nada, zip........ I could even take it a step further and tell you that I was the least handy person on the planet. I'm using solar energy because it has always been one of my goals. I also get a kick out of seeing amps and volts coming into my system just because the sun is out. It's a similar feeling to picking a tomato in your own garden or eating a fresh trout you just caught. By the way, amps tells me how fast energy is being put in or removed from the batteries. Voltage gives me an approximation of how charged the batteries are, especially at the extremes of fully charged versus almost empty.

Even though I now know much more than when I started, I am still learning every day. I recommend, unless you have superb electrician skills, that you hire someone who can help you hook up your alternative energy source.

I would like to give you a perspective regarding alternative energy. Many military Generals and Homeland Security representatives have reported how fragile America's electric grid situation has become. Just imagine, whether it be through cyber terrorism or an electromagnetic pulse (solar or man made), what life would be like if most of our electric grid went down; At the risk of being graphic, the outcome would be catastrophic. Commerce would come to a dead halt until some form of barter has been created. Food and supplies would be non-existent especially in urban America, or anywhere where the human to natural resource ratio is compromised. Let's face it, most urban grocery stores stock food for a mere 3 days. When that is gone, how will they re-order or ship without power or communication?

Until America brings back the skills that made our country great the outcome of this scenario could be awful. If I had to describe it in a short sentence it would be "murder, rape and mayhem."

Do you remember hurricane Katrina? I have talked to people who were in that area during the disaster. It was just as I described above unfortunately, the "old media" didn't broadcast the truth. Food and water were especially compromised because there was no way to prevent contamination or spoilage in such a warm climate. If this scenario happened to the whole country, use a multiplier of 10,000 times the havoc of hurricane Katrina.

This should be an incentive for every American to think and prepare with foresight and work to improve skills which would provide basic needs for survival. I promise you one thing, that if America's electric grid does go down for more than two months no one would be discussing the topics that have distracted many Americans in the past, such as how big is your home, what car you drive, where you vacation, fancy restaurants, fancy clothes, shopping for "sport", getting your hair and nails done, and even retirement. Topics like affirmative action and quotas will be dead.

If this scenario happens your life, in just two short months, would turn into "survival mode" only. Topics of discussion would include clean and uncontaminated food and water, self defense and getting away from the masses of people. I'm not trying to instill fear in anyone through subjective, emotional opinions. I'm just laying out the facts, no electric power means no America as we know it. If American's acquired the skills mentioned in this book, there would be much less disruption and the potential for greater peace and synergy.

Look at this from a different perspective. Let's say America stays "on top", the middle class prospers and everything is hunky-dory for the next 50 years. What skills are we leaving to the next generation? Skills on how to manage paper? Push buttons? Go to the grocery store? Call the electrician? What if transformers go down?

Here are some of the specifics you will need if you would like to set up your own power source. This could mean a backup power system for your existing home or you may feel the need to change your lifestyle by living off grid.

I also hear that a lot of people are disgusted by the "smart meters" being installed in their homes without their consent. What's the matter, don't you want the "powers that be" knowing your every move? What appliances you use and when you use them? When you're home and when you're not home? What about the negative health impacts of their signals?

Specific alternative energy tools

I am going to attempt to make this as simple as possible. Please don't take that statement as being condescending, but this could be the most complicated chapter to most people. I use several tools in my alternative solar energy set up. The first, and most important, are batteries. Then there are solar panels, a solar controller, a tri-metric, a DC disconnect, an inverter and a generator all wired in unison.

Let's talk first about batteries. The size of the battery bank determines how long the AC loads will operate in a backup mode without sunshine or utility power. The bigger your battery bank, the longer the run time and the longer the recharge time. Most people will tell you not to discharge your batteries more than 50%. I try to make that number 20%. Plus, when you use additional DC charging devices such as solar, wind, hydro etc., you can have longer run times because your batteries will not need AC utility or generator power. This is where your research will be paramount.

I recommend sizing your battery bank to your power usage and lifestyle. For example, one barometer to determine the size of your battery bank can be how often you will need to run your generator during the shortest days of the year. I will run my generator around two times per week during the heart of the winter and use no more than 4 gallons of gas per week during that three month stretch. That's 16 gallons of gas per month at say $4.00 per gallon; so during my darkest, coldest months, I spend $64.00 per month for fuel. The rest of the year, I mostly run my generator to operate my well pump for water. Personally, I think gasoline should be less than $1.00 per gallon with all the oil we have on our soil but, that's another story.

I want to mention a few words about proper battery cable sizing. The diameter and length is important for safety and efficient operation. Larger diameter cables (smaller AWG number) have less voltage drop and are more efficient when transferring power to and from the batteries. If the cable is undersized (diameter too small), it could potentially overheat creating a fire danger.

Cable length is also an important consideration. Keep your cable lengths as short as possible. Longer cable runs increase resistance, thus lowering the efficiency of your system. This is especially important when running a low voltage system (12 volts), where it may be necessary to provide an oversized diameter of wire. Also use copper cables that are properly sized and length rated for the amperage of the inverter and batteries.

The most popular battery is a lead acid battery. Most people recognize this battery because it is the battery type that is used in your car or pick-up truck. These vehicle batteries are designed to supply large amounts of electricity in a short burst. In other words, your car battery can supply a great amount of current in a short amount of time if the battery is "shallow" cycled.

Another lead acid battery is the "deep" cycle battery. This is the type of battery I use for my alternative energy storage. The deep cycle battery is not meant to supply a large amount of amps in a short period of time, but instead to supply a moderate amount of amps for a long period of time. Most "off grid" power sources use deep cycle lead acid batteries. They work well, there's a lot of them, they are inexpensive, and they can handle poor maintenance.

You can use maintenance-free batteries of the lead acid design. These "sealed" batteries have certain benefits beyond being maintenance-free. They do not emit gases during a REGULAR charge and you do not have to add water to the battery cells. The negatives factors are that they are extremely expensive and if you overcharge them, they will die. Overcharging will cause them to gas and lose water and, since they are sealed, you will not be able to replace the water hence, the batteries will die. These batteries are called AGM batteries. I don't recommend these batteries for your energy storage source regarding off-grid living.

There are also sealed batteries called gel cells. They are also very expensive high-quality batteries. They are like lead acid batteries except the electrolyte is not a liquid. They have advantages but can still have the same problems of the inability to add water when conditions require overcharging. I don't recommend these batteries for your energy storage source either.

There is another battery source called nickel iron which is a high energy density battery. This battery often has a lifetime guarantee but can be challenging to use in cooler climates such as Montana. This battery needs to be in temperatures no lower than 45°F. If you have a warm place to store these batteries and can afford them, then this would be a possibility.

If your lifestyle demands a lot of energy use, then I would recommend you look into industrial style batteries. They usually come with a 20 year shelf life, and they cost about $1000 each. L-16's are probably the smallest of the industrial size batteries.

I bought 12 Trojan 105's (T-105) for about $1500 which should give me about a 10-year shelf life. This is a basic lead acid battery which requires a little maintenance. My cost is about $ 13.00 per month over that 10-year period of time.

Lead acid batteries consists of two metal plates completely submerged in a solution of sulfuric acid. The positive plate is lead dioxide and the negative plate is lead. This is the chemical state where the battery is charged. When a circuit is attached from the negative plate to the positive plate, electrons flow in what is called electric current. When electrical current flows, the battery will lose stored electrical energy.

Since most people use non-sealed, lead acid batteries, as I do, for their alternative power, I should mention that there needs to be some maintenance. First of all, you need to check the water levels (electrolytes) at least every two months. Distilled water should be used to refill the cells when they are low. Secondly, you need to take specific gravity readings of each battery cell with an accurate hydrometer. Specific gravity is a measurement of density of a liquid.

Batteries work best at 77°F. At higher temperatures they will out perform their ratings, but they will have a shorter life. In the wintertime, my batteries have an ambient temperature of about 40°F, which means they will lose approximately 10% to 15% of their capacity to store electrical energy. In the summertime, I will get 100% of their energy capacity. So, in a nutshell, batteries will perform better in warmer temperatures, but have a longer shelf life in cooler temperatures. It's a good trade off!

The exception to this is when batteries are exposed to temperatures below 32°. If they are deeply discharged, the electrolyte becomes mostly water that can freeze and break the casing and plates. When batteries get below freezing, they can lose too much of their storage capacity. These batteries will need to be charged at a higher voltage to assure they reach full charge. This is when the off grid person can get in trouble. A battery bank needs to get close to full charge at least every 7 to 8 days. For northern climates or higher elevations I recommend that a battery temperature sensor option be installed on your inverter. The sensor sits in between the batteries while the port is plugged into your inverter. This sensor will extend battery life by preventing overcharging in warm temperatures and undercharging in cold temperatures.

During periods of low sun, usually in the winter months, undercharging can be an issue. A charged battery has plates of lead and lead dioxide. When the battery is discharged, the plates are coated with lead sulfate. When the battery stays in a state of low charge for a long time, the lead sulfate coating on the plates changes from the normal lead sulfate to a crystalline lead sulfate. The crystalline lead sulfate is resistant to charging. This process is known as sulfation. This will lead to unequal specific gravity in different cells in your battery bank. When this occurs you need to charge your batteries above normal voltage for a longer period of time. This process is called equalization and should be done approximately every 60 to 90 days.

A new battery has 100% of its rated capacity. As with all batteries, capacity will decrease and deteriorate over time. When a battery reaches approximately 80% of its capacity, its life will be short. Some of the signs will be a quick charge time and a very quick discharge rate. In other words, its capacity for storing electrical energy has become very small.

When charging your batteries, especially during an equalization process, your batteries will gas more than normal. Make sure your "electronics area" is well ventilated. Batteries will give off flammable hydrogen gas so be sure to keep flames and sparks away from this area. This includes your inverter and especially your generator. I recommend storing your batteries in a box, so you can open and close the lid as necessary. I also recommend having a door to the outside to ventilate the area when running your generator. Don't try to extend an exhaust pipe from your generator. It will get too hot and most likely cause a fire.

When people discuss the size of their alternative power system, they often talk about many different units of measure. Some people mention how many solar panels they have, their wattage (my solar array consists of only eight panels with a total of 1060 Watts) and some people mention the size of their generator. The proper unit of measure to use when discussing the size or power of your solar system is "amp hours". My system is only 675 amp hours in size. Compared to most "off grid" living, this is on the small side because we live semi-rugged compared to most folks. We don't have a television set, major appliances, water heater, pressure tank, dryer (we use a foldable wood rack you can get at Lehman's) or a lot of modern conveniences. Who the heck has the time? There is too much hunting and fishing to do around here anyway!

Another important tool in my energy set up is a Tri-metric. This tool helps save valuable energy by letting me see how much I'm using. It also gives me valuable automated information so I can protect my battery investment. Plus, it gives me an opportunity to check and locate system problems when they occur.

My Tri-metric allows me the opportunity to monitor many automated readings that are applicable to the health of my energy system. For example, I can press a button and find out how many amp hours I am from "full". This is an important reading because I try not to get below 80% of "full" at any time. This diligence will keep my battery capacity and shelf life strong. So, I simply take my 675 amp hours of my system and multiply that times .20 to give me a total of 135 amps. Since the Tri-metric counts up from zero, I try not to go over 135 amps during any seven to eight day period. It's simple!

The Tri-metric also has automated readings like how many days ago since the batteries were last fully charged, how many days since they were equalized, and maximum and minimum battery voltage. I can reset my Tri-metric battery system monitor to many different settings that measure battery care, energy conservation, system maintenance measures, battery voltage, amps and amp hours. I even use this tool to check for "phantom loads". This is when I forget to unplug something in my cabin that will still draw amps out of my battery bank. A printer, television, microwave, VCR or DVD player are notorious for using amps even though they aren't turned on. (A printer is the only one I have on this list). This phenomenon can also be responsible for setting homes on fire.

The Tri-metric will affect the life of your battery bank and two actions on your part are critical. Programming your equipment with proper voltage set points and frequently recharging your battery bank to a full state of charge, (remember every 7 to 8 days). I recommend this tool for every alternative power set up, but, if you don't check specific gravity readings regularly, your Tri-metric will "lie" to you. Calculations and readings must correlate to accurate battery health.

The next important tool is a solar controller. I have what's called a TriStar by Morningstar corporation. The purpose of the solar controller is so I can charge my batteries from the sun and at the same time prevent my batteries from overcharging. This tool is also automated and has many settings. I can even equalize my battery bank with this tool.

Next on the list of necessary equipment is the inverter/charger. This tool will convert my AC power from my generator and store it as DC power in my batteries. Additionally, all of my stored DC power, that has come from my solar array into my batteries, will now be transferred back through the inverter into my cabin for AC power usage.

The inverter uses extremely low current while in the "search" mode, consuming less than 1 watt of power. In the "on" mode the inverter/ charger uses less than 12 watts of power. This is very low power usage. An inverter can support either a 12, 24 or a 48 volt battery bank depending on the model. I use a 24-volt system.

The inverter has a built in charger and a three-stage charging process to maintain the batteries, these are bulk, absorption and float charges. The bulk stage is the first stage in the charging process and provides the batteries with a controlled constant current. The second stage is the absorption charge. During this stage the current supplied to the batteries slowly decreases. The third stage is the float charge. The float charge is a very low current charge which is also called a trickle charge.

I also use what is called a DC Disconnect and Over Current Protection. In its simplest definition, it is to isolate the batteries and protect the solar controller. Fuses and other disconnects must be sized to protect the wiring in the system. The National Electrical Code requires both over current protection and a disconnect switch for residential and commercial electrical systems.

Last but not least is a generator. I use a 7000 watt generator that has a 240 volt hookup for just about any tool a household could use indoors or outdoors. This way I don't have to wire my cabin for 240 volts indoors. I have a 120 volt hookup inside my cabin and this keeps life simple. My generator takes gasoline and I use the best premium, non-ethanol fuel. In fact, I use this type of gas on all of my tools. I chose a gas generator because all of my tools that aren't run by electricity are run by gasoline. This includes my chainsaw, wood splitter, UTV (this is a side by side ATV), and my pick up truck. The generator has a Honda engine which is rated high for performance and shelf life. If you change your oil on a regular basis, as I do, you can expect many good years of healthy generator usage. By the way, I prefer synthetic oil for the generator.

The most important job the generator has is to pull up water from a one horse power pump I have submerged in my well. My well is 250 feet deep with a static water level of 40 feet. Static water level is where the water "settles" after digging a well. So every time I run the generator to get water, I am also "banking" amps and voltage into my system, (killing two birds with one stone).

There are other alternative sources of power besides solar. The most commonly used after solar is wind energy. Here in northwest Montana we just don't get a lot of wind. That's okay by me because I do not like high winds. Wind energy isn't as functional or efficacious as solar. Because, you need to be in a place where you get a lot of wind to justify its set up.

Another source of energy is hydro energy. I know a few people who have it and it works great. The two main considerations are enough water volume and local and state regulations. Regarding water volume, you need a certain volume of water to drop at a certain rate to provide you with proper amps and voltage. Secondly, government regulations can be a tricky deterrent as well. In most places of the country, surface water is often heavily regulated. Even though I "own" half of the river that runs through my property, water rights are still an issue. I do know of a family who has an under ground spring with enough volume and drop to produce excellent electricity, but that's a rare case.

I want to discuss some of the monetary benefits of producing your own power. I have to admit, making my own power has always been a goal of mine and it's a lot of fun, and the money-saving rewards are obvious. My whole system, every tool I mentioned in this chapter, including the electrical hookups (done by a professional) cost me approximately $15,000. Now, let's put this into perspective. If I were to hook up to the "corporate electric grid", my bill would be a minimum of $40,000 to pull in power. Not to mention the fact that I would be hooked up to a "smart meter" and would be paying a fortune in monthly bills.

Let's look at this a different way. My solar panels may lose 1% of efficiency per year, at most. So, odds are, since I'm 53 years old, I will probably not have to change out any of my solar panels (and that's assuming I live to 85). Besides, solar panels are pretty cheap these days. Electric devices such as an inverter, Tri-metric, charge controller and even my generator could die. So far, knock on wood, six years of living off grid has been pretty simple and I have been using the same electronic devices since the beginning. The only item that you will replace, for sure, are the batteries. I spent about $1500 for 12 batteries that should last me for approximately 10 years.

Remember, I told you that the majority of middle-class Americans spend their disposable income on food, energy and entertainment/recreation. It's up to you how you spend your money. You can give it to the corporate electric companies every month or spend it one time on your own personal power grid and have a lot more free time to go hunting and fishing.

This chapter would be too long to include any more specifics. Just like the other chapters in this book, it's up to you to read the basics I'm describing and then research your own options. I can tell you that making my own power has a lot of benefits and rewards. Keep in mind that the technology is here! We are not using candles and kerosene lanterns as mandatory sources of lighting these days. It doesn't matter which state you set up your self-sufficient home, all 50 states have rural areas. Yes, even Jersey!

Relearn our 19th century skills, but use 21st century technology when available.

Another alternative energy source being used in America is hydrogen. This is being used very quietly because it is a free energy source and the "powers that be" cannot make money from the people. There are people running lawn mowers, cars, generators and homes off this gas. It's fuel is basically water and it's emission is oxygen. If this energy source went viral it would make our planet a virtual garden over night and give independence and freedom to the world.

Good source of information and solar products: Backwoods Solar, Sandpoint ID. www.backwoodssolar.com

(208) 263-2490

This is a cool book for simplifying your life: Lehman's non-electric catalog www.lehmans.com

A good fictional read about a grid down scenario in the US, - "One Second After" by William R. Fortchen.

"Patriots", a novel of survival of the coming collapse by James Wesley Rawles.

Chapter 14 - Edible and Medicinal plants

Since I am privileged to live in the heart of mother nature country, I try and utilize the tools and resources offered to me. I concentrate on harvesting wild edible and medicinal plants that are immune stimulants and plants that reduce inflammation in bones and joints. This is especially important for someone like myself who has spinal stenosis and nerve damage. I also concentrate on plants that fight cancer and reduce or eliminate tumors. And of course, I will also pick a plant just because I'm hungry or it tastes great.

One of the last radio shows on which I was a guest, was an overview of what type of land to purchase regarding a self-sufficient lifestyle. Plenty of questions were sent my way after the show but, believe it or not, the majority of the responses I received were in "awe", just because of one specific statement that I made. I simply said that during six months of the year, here, "you can walk behind me with a bottle of salad dressing and you will never go hungry." This tells me that too many Americans have only one plan of action and that is the grocery store. It doesn't matter if the food is GMO, synthetic, artificial, refined or processed. (Remember my personal acronym SARP.) It doesn't matter if they don't know where the food comes from or who picked it. It doesn't even matter how much they are paying for it or if it is organic. It could be laced with pesticides and they would still buy it. People are hungry for not just healthy food but good information as well. I can write a book on just edible plants but, again, this overall book is targeted to give the American people reasons and examples on why we should live a more self-sufficient lifestyle.

First, I would like to start with some edible plants that I have on my property. I want to make this point very clear: edible plants are almost everywhere. It's up to you to do your research, due diligence and educate yourself on what mother nature has to offer. Here, on just my property alone, I have about ten different species of edible berries. This list includes wild strawberries, raspberries, oregon grape, current, gooseberries, service berries, choke cherries, hawthorne berries, kinnikinnick berries and buffalo berries. Buffalo berry is very unpalatable and should be used for emergency food only. I often make a joke that if you eat to much buffalo berry you need to have a small dog nearby so you can lick its ass in order to get the taste out of your mouth.

We also go to higher elevations and harvest our share of huckleberries and elderberries. Huckleberries are definitely the best tasting berry I have ever picked. Elderberry was probably the best tasting wine we have ever made. Yes, we do make some homemade wine every year and, as you can imagine, it's very rewarding. By the way, wild raw berries (especially blue in color) in general are potent anti-tumor agents (anti-oxidants). Wild berries are very useful and versatile-did you know that gin can be made out of juniper berries? They are also a good pepper substitute.

What's nice about having such a variety of berries is the fact that they're all maturing at different times in the spring, summer and fall. We pick the strawberries and raspberries in late spring and early summer and the oregon grape and kinnikinnick are picked around September to October.

We also harvest mushrooms; we concentrate on only two types because of their outstanding taste. The first is called the morel mushroom and there are two types which we harvest. One grows on the river bottoms and another grows a year after a fire. (What I mean is that we pick these mushrooms the next summer after a fire goes through a specific area the previous year.) The second species of mushroom that grows all over my property in the fall, is called shaggy manes. They need to be picked as soon as possible because they get soft and "inky" if left in the ground too long. These mushrooms are delicious but, they unfortunately have a very short lifespan and shelflife.

In the spring when everything is starting to grow, I also harvest some wild greens to add to our salad. Our salad usually has lettuce, spinach, swiss chard, carrots, radishes and asparagus. The wild greens that are added to this mix include red clover, violets/pansies, fire weed, raspberry blight, oxeye daisies, lambs ear, dandelion and wild onion.

Red Clover has long been considered a blood purifier and the whole plant can be eaten. It helps the liver and body eliminate waste materials from the blood and it has also been known to help thin the blood. Red clover also contains anti-tumor qualities too.

The flowers and leaves of wild violet/pansy plant can be eaten and are excellent sources of vitamin C and A. I've even read where they can calm the nerves of people under stress. By the way, if you ever get called a "pansy", look at it as a compliment. The wild violet pansies that grow on my place are the first to appear in the spring, as early as February, and the last to die off, sometimes as late as early December. They are tough plants and the most adaptable wild flower I know.

Fire weed is high in chlorophyll and can aid in anemic conditions. I like to pick the fire weed leaves and young shooting tips in the spring. I often refer to this young plant as a "poor man's asparagus."

Raspberry blight is often referred to as strawberry blight depending on your resource manual. This plant is related to spinach and I usually add a very small amount of this to my salad. Because it can contain high amounts of oxalic acid. This plant is a good source of vitamins B and C and has a high iron content, just like spinach.

Oxeye daisy leaves help with sciatic pain by reducing uric acid in the blood. I harvest some of these young leaves when they first pop out of the soil in the spring.

Dandelions, now who in America doesn't have these wonderful edible plants popping up all spring and summer? You can eat the roots, leaves and flowers. The dandelion leaves are high in vitamin C and calcium. This plant can relieve the body of excess uric acid and helps conditions such as arthritis. Oh and don't forget, dandelion makes an excellent wine! Some words of wisdom, be careful when harvesting these or any plants on other people's property. Always check to see if the land owner sprayed poison first.

Wild onion, do I need to say anymore? It grows abundantly here in Northwest Montana and can be eaten right out of the ground. It tastes sweet and there is no bitter taste at all. Make sure it smells like an onion because it can look similar to what's called death camas. As you can tell by it's name it is toxic.

Many plants have some edible and medicinal benefits, and nature has purposely made different berries and plants to mature at different times of the year-just like the vegetables in your garden which contain different fruits, greens and roots. Don't fight nature! Take advantage of nature's variety out in the forest.

The cold of winter is our "free energy" refrigerator. We leave our food on the basement floor, by the outside door, where it stays a constant 35 to 40°. This way we do not have to run the small refrigerator all winter long. We leave our perishable food on the floor from early November to late March. We get the bulk of the electricity we use from the end of February to end of October via solar power. We start gardening in late March and usually go into early November. The point is that our lifestyle doesn't fight the seasons but, we work with the seasons. So if a plant that you want isn't normally available at a certain time of year, make a plan to preserve it for next year! Use what you have available during that specific time of year for your advantage.

Here's another health analogy. Let's say you are in a lot of physical pain and you sleep very poorly. If you take the same sleeping pill over and over, every day, your body will eventually resist that molecule. You need to fake out your body, every now and then, because the efficacy of that sleeping pill will just decrease over time. The same holds true for edible and medicinal plants and this is why nature rotates the maturity of all plants. I think it is wise to not take the same plants every day, 365 days per year. You need to know what harm these plants could do to your liver and kidneys. Some plants can be eaten every day but some are very toxic. It's your job to do the research. This book isn't to prescribe or diagnose or to be a substitute for an accredited professional health caregiver. The purpose is to motivate you to seek new information that is out there in nature.

Speaking of sleep deprivation. I will, once in a while take a wild plant for sleep. This plant has worked much better than any of the sleeping pills I have ever taken from the pharmaceutical industry. This plant is called Skullcap. Some manuals also name it as Helmet flower, Hoodwart, and Quaker bonnet. This plant can be used for insomnia and nerve pain...... which is right up my alley. So I get a double whammy benefit! I get the opportunity to have my spine and arm pain slightly decreased while becoming somewhat sleepy. To my knowledge, this plant doesn't have any side effects. It will not make you high, or will make you feel drowsy the next day.

This plant can be combined with Valerian (This plant has similar medicinal benefits to Skullcap) and Willow to create a safe pain relief formula. (Did you know that Willow bark can be used as aspirin when chewed on? Our pioneers and American Indians knew that fact.) Skullcap can be used for other medicinal uses but, my incentives are for insomnia and pain.

We make a tincture out of skullcap by putting it in a dark-colored glass jar and adding water and a little bit of Everclear alcohol to help with preservation. We then let it sit in a dark area, for two weeks and it is ready for use. We will transfer several days of dosages into a smaller dark colored glass and take several drops from an eyedropper. There are many books available on making tinctures.

As I have mentioned, everything should be used in moderation and never for long term use. In Chapter 11, I briefly discussed a tea I harvest from the forest. I mentioned that I felt this tea was possibly responsible for the reduction in the size of my lymph nodes. The name of this "dry" forest mushroom is chaga. Chaga contains massive amounts of the enzyme superoxide dismutase (SOD), which is rarely found in any edible substances. This enzyme will absorb noxious free radicals before they can damage the body. Chaga contains 25 to 50 times more SOD than any other medicinal mushroom. Do you remember reading about the early 1900's when people were ending sickness by eating moldy bread? Voila, penicillin: a mold, and a new medicinal invention which destroyed many an infection. Chaga creates a strong body and enhances the immune system. The immune system deals with inflammation, circulation, allergies, infections, detoxification and the prevention of tumors and cancer.

Chaga is best harvested from birch trees. Chaga is rich in nutrients and may be considered one of the worlds top sources of minerals and vitamins. It contains virtually every known nutrient except for vitamins A and K and is an excellent source of B vitamins. Vitamin B-12 is well-known in prophylactic therapy for fighting cancer.

Wild Chaga is high in antioxidants as are the bark and buds of the white birch tree. (Be careful of people growing this substance in laboratories-it's proven to not have much efficacy.) I use the bark and buds for fighting pain and inflammation. The best specimens are of northern varieties. Where the winters can be harsh so the anticancer/anti-tumor properties will be stronger. For example, the birch bark has two main substances; betulin and betulinic acid, both of which are excellent cancer fighters.

Larch/Tamarack bark will directly inhibit the enzyme xanthine oxidase. This enzyme is responsible for making uric acid, which may lead to the formation of urate crystals. These crystals will deposit in joints and lead to gout attacks. Larch bark contains a lot of nutrients including minerals, B vitamins and vitamin C. I will also, on occasion, put some larch bark in my tea.

I often add rose hips to my tea as well. In the late fall, after the bloom of the wild rose has faded, I will harvest the rose hips. These are the little round seeds that are left over after the rose dies. They're a great source of vitamin C plus a good food source when hunting in the fall. Don't forget to add wild violets because the flowers and leaves of the wild plant are excellent sources of vitamin C and A.

I want to take a moment to discuss something that I'm sure some of you are thinking about in the back of your minds: medical marijuana. I'm sure I now have your undivided attention. This topic gives me mixed emotions because I do believe in our Constitution, freedoms and liberties. I do believe that we should be able to do what we want, in the privacy of our own homes and on our own land, with the company of consenting adults. However, I do feel that when people abuse those rights and start to kill people then those rights should be taken away from that specific individual and only that specific individual. For example, if you take any chemical and drive a vehicle and then kill someone, your rights should be suspended or lost. This goes for marijuana, alcohol, prescription drugs (especially anti-psychotics and I feel the pharmaceutical industry and doctors should be liable) or any other drug or naturally occurring chemical which is voluntarily taken.

I have personally tried medically prescribed marijuana and it did not help my pain or improve my sleep. I'm not saying it doesn't help anyone, I'm just saying it didn't benefit me. Personally, I don't like any drug that is mind altering. The only exception would be if a person is in extreme pain. I know I have said that nature and everything natural is the best feeling in the world. The exception to that rule, again, for me is mind altering drugs. If you take them in your home and have zero probability of killing someone, then it's a different story. (This is just my opinion). Just remember, this drug phenomenon craze is purposely part of the plan to reduce the population and keep as many people as possible from being "thinkers." The more mindless followers America has, the lower the life expectancy, prosperity and quality of life for future middle class Americans. These examples hold even more water for Meth. I don't know how anyone can live in a place like this, with so much beauty and adventure and take that drug...or any drug, especially if your young and healthy. I just don't get it!

I have really struggled on how to deliver this information on edible and medicinal plants. My initial notes found me writing another book on the topic. Another dilemma was the fact that edible and medicinal plants are often regional regarding benefits and species. I have several books at home that I follow that are mostly regional plants of the West and Northwest. As with most of my "how-to" chapters, I have found that motivating people to get them to the next step is the best way. I could mention dozens of edible and medicinal plants but it wouldn't benefit you especially if the plants are not found in your area. It's up to you to broaden your horizon and find books and websites specific to your area of the country. It's fairly easy to do the research and educate yourself on the benefits of these great gifts from nature's God.

I will close out this chapter by sharing a family story about my grandmother. During WW11, she was put in a concentration camp by Stalin. She was in this concentration camp for nearly 20 years. My grandmother told my mother that the only reason she survived was because she knew how to harvest wild edible plants.

When Stalin died, that concentration camp was disbanded and my grandmother was set free. My father wrote then VP Richard Nixon who contacted Khrushchev in a letter explaining the circumstances and requested help in re-uniting the family. Nixon, as per my mother, called my Dad to confirm this story over the phone. My grandmother was found, thanks to Nixon, and was able to legally immigrate to America to be united with my mom. My grandmother lived to 86 years old because she knew how to harvest edible plants in the forest!

I will recommend a couple of good books for people who live in the West.

Edible and Medicinal Plants of the West, by Gregory L. Tilford

The Forest Farmacy, by Thomas J. Tracey – This is a great book written by a local herbalist from Bigfork, Mt.

Natural Remedies Encyclopedia, by Vance Ferrell and Harold M. Cherne, M.D.

E.C. Kraus-Home Wine and Beer Making Supplies www.eckraus.com

Midwest Supplies- Home Brewing and Wine Making www.midwestsupplies.com

Chapter 15: How about this idea!

About two or three years ago there was a "Preparedness/Self-Sufficiency" Expo in Kalispell, Montana. It was a very successful Expo with a lot of interesting exhibits and curious consumers looking for a Plan "B" because they had so much fear regarding our economy and their future.

I was one of the speakers at this Expo and there was a lot of interest; people had to sit on the floor or stand because all of the seats were taken. My topic of discussion was "from Metropolitan life to living off grid in northwest Montana." There were definitely many people who wanted a choice for alternative living and who wanted information on how to have a better and simpler lifestyle. In particular, they were interested in reducing their bills, eating healthier foods, having a little more space, privacy and nature around them. In other words, they were just looking for a better quality of life so they could control a larger portion of their own destiny.

The Expo was a lot of fun because quite a few people, some of whom are friends today, continue to follow-up with many more questions. It's amazing how many people in the middle-class have lost their ability to retire, increase their home equity, their desire to save for the future and their dreams. I feel that this lifestyle is not only rewarding but can enhance certain skills that will restore Americans' hope. Under the situation that we have presently (which includes wealth redistribution and jobs to people who have victim/protectionist group status, being bombarded by all sorts of political correctness, offering huge paychecks and pensions to government and union employees) there is no way that a major devaluation of our quality of life will not continue to occur. I mean the devaluation of everything that made America great; family, college educations, quality of our food and water, savings and investments; real estate values (especially urban/suburban homes and commercial properties) and the American dollar etc. Working hard just has lost a lot of it's benefits over the years.

So, if we keep printing money that deflates the Dollars value, what are we offering our future generations? This is where my idea comes in to play. If every barometer of economic growth and success is blurred and corrupted what is our plan? If 90% of college degrees are practically worthless, what do we do? Not to mention the debt our young adults have after they graduate. There aren't even enough jobs to go around for our youth today never mind the rest of the population. Especially, with all these regulations. Companies and American people would rather leave the country rather than lose all their money to the angry hoards of attorney's in this country. A country where people with "victim group status" sue at a drop of a hat. A law suit for a "joke in the hallway" or even a compliment on their fitness level or attire. It's ridiculous!

Before I give specific examples of my idea, I need to put a few things in context. First, the "powers that be" are only feathering their own nests. Every American can write a book about all of the bailouts that have occurred over the past 15 years....mainly to the super wealthy. Bailouts to banks, insurance companies, auto companies, solar companies, Wall Street and government spending....................... The way I see it, all of the bailout recipients are basically governments workers. This includes thousands of CEO's and executives, too. If I wrote them all down it would be a book on its own.

I also know of very wealthy people who own 5,000 to 150,000 acres who have received government money to develop springs and wells for their cattle, on their personal ranches. Some of these ranchers have received more money in government grants than any 500 welfare, food stamp and WIC recipients put together. I have noticed, in most cases, that the people who receive the most money are often the people who have the most assets and wealth-go figure!

I have also noticed that the people working for the government have an easy time distributing other people's money; with no consequences to themselves. In fact, they often get "favors" in return. It's especially noticeable when the big money distribution goes from the government 'powers that be" to their buddies, including their private sector buddies. Maybe, we should have a law that you only take from the kitty when you put into that specific kitty or pot.

So if all this phony, non-tangible paper wealth redistribution keeps occurring while causing negative changes to the wealth of American middle class, what is our plan? What is going to have value in the future?

Here is a partial solution! We need to get back to the skills, traditions, heritage and culture that made America great. We need to eliminate the majority of the government programs and redistribute the money so Americans can acquire the skills that will ensure their future. These monies need to go to the middle class and poor, not the super wealthy "buddies" and "special interest groups."

We need to start preparedness/self-sufficiency schools across America. We need to provide an incentive to people who enroll in a school that will enhance the skills of future generations. We do not need more people in banks distributing money via fractional reserve lending. We do not need more people on Wall Street selling non-tangible worthless paper. We do not need the federal reserve printing more money and buying back our own debt. We do not need our Treasury Department issuing more IOU's. We need America to open its eyes to the phony, white-collar, suit and tie propaganda. We need to relearn the skills that made America great.

If the American government invested in more trade schools and less in "University" type schools, we would have a brighter future. Fewer young people would be unemployed. They would realize that tangible assets hold much more value than a piece of paper. (Paper could include stocks, bonds, ETF's etc.) We could have a country where equality is measured by hard work, effort, proven results, qualifications, word of honor, diligence, tenacity and principal. We could have a country where the poor and middle class have similar life expectancies as the rich.

Despite having graduated from three different colleges, I am now a huge proponent of trade schools. We need to change the mentality about education to boost enrollment in America's trade schools. Even in the little town where I reside in northwest Montana, there is a need for good trade skills. One example is vehicle mechanics. A good mechanic can pull in to any state and most towns and get a job or start a business in a few days.

So let's put our government money into useful skills. Let's teach our youth how to fish so we don't have to give them a fish to eat everyday. Especially early in life, none of our youth in this country should ever be out of work. Being self-sufficient creates more pride, greater work ethic and more independent thinking.

The million-dollar question is, do the "powers that be" want to allow the masses to think again? Do they want the masses of "sheeple" to be herded into the cities to be their controlled slaves? Do they want to create a collapse in order to initiate Martial law and eliminate our Constitution? Have they "collateralized" our Federal and State lands and people because of their immense spending? Are these introduced wolves here to eliminate our food so the poorer, more self-sufficient people can be more controlled? (How do you think they destroyed and then controlled the American Indian? They killed the buffalo, which was their main food source, then controlled them.) Is history repeating itself? Mull that over for a while.

This preparedness/self-sufficiency school idea can include some of the following topics. I feel that most of our high school and even college graduates are severely lacking in these areas. Here are some examples of subjects that could be offered to individuals and families alike.

-Living off grid-This lifestyle would teach people about nature, self sufficiency, and frugality. It will give today's youth an opportunity to see where food comes from and the "real, tangible" importance of life. Rural real estate alone would contribute so much positive real growth to our GDP.

-Alternative energy-This would teach people how to set up their own power source.

-Buying land- We could show Americans the micro and macro benefits to buying tangible land. Where to buy and how to buy land. Buying land with 401(k)s or IRAs, in other words pretax money. Their would be a new excitement in America. Land, especially 20 acres or more rarely goes into foreclosure, however they are always making houses in subdivisions.

-Raising animals- Teach people about which animals are the most practical and efficient. Best food producing animals. How to pick healthy animals. How to feed, care and house them. How to breed them and identify common diseases. How to prepare different kinds of food utilizing animals. (eggs, milk, butter, meat, etc.)

-Hunting, fishing- Teach hunting and fishing strategies. How to skin & butcher animals.

-Canning- How to can and preserve your foods.

-Hand gun defense- I spent a week in Nevada last year at a hand gun defense class. I was amazed at how many people were there during the week just for this training and seeing the desire to learn these skills was very encouraging. This training also gives gun owners a credited gun handling course under their belts. This course will prevent the gun "naysayers" from trying to eliminate our second amendment rights. The name of this specific school in Nevada is called Front Site.

-Our Constitution- We need to teach and reteach the Constitution and Bill of Rights to the American people. Too many Americans, over time, have given their lives to preserve the rights guaranteed in our constitution. We owe this to our fallen heroes or it will all have been for naught. The Constitution is the foundation of our country and our government.

-Financial counseling and our economy- It's amazing to me how many Americans do not even know what is an amortization schedule. We need to teach buyers of homes, land and businesses where to put their money. We need to teach them the difference between principal and interest. They need to understand what is equity. I am even more shocked when today's high school graduates do not know how to balance a checkbook. There are lots of basic financial principles and simple accounting that would promote prosperity to Americans in this category.

-Wild edible and medicinal plants- This would teach Americans survival skills in case of an economic catastrophe. Botany and nature should be appreciated by everyone.

- Nutrition- Most Americans have no clue! I keep thinking about some visitors we had this summer from New York City. One of them was a young boy who had no idea about nutrition. The subject of Doritos came up and he went back home with a different perspective. I shared with him the fact that Doritos could be a excellent survival "food", but not for eating. I shared with him about all of the chemicals in these artificial chips. He didn't believe me when I told him that Doritos can be used as a great fire starter. If you don't believe me light a match to one and see what happens! There are similar effects from Fritos corn chips as well. After this education, this young boy threw the whole bag of Doritos into the fire.

- Homeschooling ideas- I know there are exceptions to the rule, as with most rules, but this exception happens rarely. I can confidently say that most home schooled children I have met have a better work ethic, are more timely, have better communication skills and much better listening skills than their public school counterparts. My personal observation, regarding listening skills, I have noticed that the better the listening skills, the sooner that individual is debt free in life. People can be taught to create their own community schools based on popular curriculum for their region. It would be 1000 times less expensive than today's public schools. No tenure, extreme high pay or pensions and more accountability. OR would you rather have your kids and grand kids enrolled in "common core". Look it up if you care.

- Gardening and Farming- These were the life-lines of our pioneer and homesteader ancestors. People used this knowledge to stay alive and thrive and now we need to use this knowledge to stay healthy and avoid the over abundance of chemicals on our grocery store shelves.

Maybe this idea could move into a TV show someday for the "new media" on the Internet. This should be a show that teaches Americans self sufficiency skills. Maybe we can also have a show that reveres people who try and help others in lieu of showing giant houses and lists of the richest people in the world.

As I am writing this, I am listening to the news on the "new media". This program reported about a study that just got approval in America that will cost us well over six figures. Are you ready for this? This study is about why American lesbians are so overweight. If you don't believe me, look it up! It was just mentioned on the Wilkow Majority program.

If you're afraid to stand for something you will fall for everything! Don't just listen to the ideologies, pay attention to the people who have the ideas and the guts to implement them.

Chapter 16: Some Final Thoughts

Political correctness has dominated American culture and is nothing more than a blunt, intentional indoctrination into a social agenda to keep the super rich wealthy and everyone else in the just getting by "category". This is the great transfer of wealth from our middle class.

Let's say that we met 30 years ago and I told you many facts, as I have mentioned quite a few in this book, about what would be happening today in 2013. Some of these facts would include the NDAA and that we are debating if it's okay to kill Americans with drones without due process of the law. Discussions about gun confiscation and torture. The NSA spying on their own people. The IRS targeting conservative people and having "other" government departments doing the investigation (that's letting the fox guard the hen-house). How about our Congress publicly saying that we should "pass the bill and read what's in it later." The "left" targeting conservative leaders by trying to entrap them by putting child pornography on their computers. The "powers that be" attacking honest whistle blowers, trying to help America, instead of corrupt bankers. How about Benghazi, no rescue for an attack on our own people? Are you kidding me? Sorry, I lost it for a second there. Don't forget "fast and furious"?

So, say it's 1983 and I'm from the future and I laid out the step-by-step catastrophes, loss of traditions and culture that would happen by 2013. I would mention our (60 something percent) divorce rate. The fact that almost 50% of our babies being born in America are out of wedlock. Or how many kids in their twenties and thirties who are still living with their mommy and daddy, or because of our estranged culture should I just say mommy's. I would mention our obesity and drug use numbers.... I would mention all of the corruption in our financial and governmental institutions. I would mention everything that has happened regarding our financial, economic, political and social agendas. What would you say after I was done talking? You know that you would call me the biggest pessimistic, negative liar in the world. You would walk away in disbelief and say "that guy was crazy." When I mention this scenario in a talk or in a one-on-one conversation with someone, they always agree that you don't even have to go back 30 years. They say this disbelief would be the same if the time span were only five or ten years. What a shame!

If our country continues to make political correctness our "God" then your kids and grand kids will never be free. They will be told what to say and not to say, what to do and how to do it and who to do it with; how to think and how to live and, maybe even someday, if we can keep striving towards this great notion of equality, maybe all of us will be told where to live as well. In fact, most of us can see this very sad trend of the masses being herded into urban/suburban America, just like sheep or maybe horses. Think about this analogy, your on a mountain top overlooking a beautiful, wild herd of happy and healthy horses. They are running and playing everywhere, eating a well balanced diet because they have thousands of acres to roam. You see a couple of cowboys trying to chase these horses so they can catch them, use them and sell them. They are unsuccessful every time and the horses keep getting away. One day these cowboys start feeding these horses in one spot for months and then they build a fence. Soon the fences are built more narrow to move the horses in areas where they have less room to breath (like our cities.) Before the horses could figure out what has happened they are pushed in a tiny little area where they are easily loaded into a truck and controlled for the rest of their lives. Will these horses ever be able to control their diet, recreation, exercise or jobs ever again?

Have you ever asked yourself, why follow so many people who don't practice what they preach? They say to live green but they don't live that way themselves. They say "do it for the kids",while they get rich off of the taxpayer dollars! These people use more jet fuel, electricity, water and taxpayer dollars than anyone else on the planet. I use less than 200 gallons of water every 8 to 12 days. When I was working as a pharmaceutical rep, I would use that much hot water during one shower, just on my spine to help relieve some pain before driving for the day.

Do you think these big mouths out of Washington D.C. are making any sacrifices? Of course not! So how can you follow anyone who has no accountability or has a special tier of accountability for words and actions? How can you follow anyone who spends other peoples' money without facing any consequences?

Are you afraid of being politically incorrect or being on a list? I've got news for you, we are all on a list and they are very sophisticated. I know people who can't even go to Canada because they had a DUI 40 years ago. A DUI isn't even a felony.

Just follow the laws of our Constitution and you will be right and they will be wrong every time! If our Constitution goes down then books like this one will be illegal because free speech will be one of the first rights to go. Telling the truth will be breaking the law. Truth will only be interpreted by the elite who will control all mediums and media. Will you be satisfied with that? If you see the "powers that be" rallying to control the internet-it's over!

Until the people address the truth and eliminate political correctness from all facets of life then you, America's poor and middle-class will continue to lose ground. You will be the experiments and the "hobby farm" of the elites. Remember the saying "no guts, no glory"? It's now time to put aside personal glory; now it's time to say "no guts, no freedom". There is no more time for being subtle. It's your choice!

I'm going to ask a favor from you, the reader. I want you to make this book about you and your choices, dreams, goals and lifestyle. I don't want you to make this book about me. I wrote this book so that the unfortunate circumstances I went through may not happen to you; and that the successes I've had, for my humble dreams, may happen to you in a similar way. I've tried my best to share the true facts about what is happening in America today. I honestly told the economic, financial, political and social reasons why self-sufficiency and tangibility should be discussed at every dinner table.

I hope different people have enjoyed this book for different reasons. I hope some are intrigued by a self-sufficient/frugal/off-grid lifestyle. Maybe some were motivated by the outdoor adventures and living with nature. I hope some people can use this information to create a path for their own lifestyle changes. I hope some are motivated and inspired to not give up on themselves or their dreams, goals or health. I hope some realize that we as a people need to draw a line in the sand and have ZERO tolerance for political correctness. If we don't have the same rules, laws and accountability for everyone on American soil, we will be a conquered American people.

I hope the biggest subset of people who can benefit from this book are the 90% who live in urban/suburban America. I hope that some of you have realized that a life in nature can be so wonderful and rewarding. For what's left of the middle class, this may be your last bastion of paradise and hope where you can control at least some of your own destiny. My 27 years in Montana have been a glorious outdoor adventure; my outdoor adventure life is a cross-section between the 1970's movies The Wilderness Family, Dr. Doolittle and Jeremiah Johnson. It's a life where common sense and logic actually have relevance. I don't have to worry about keeping up with the Jones', wearing a suit and tie anymore, or even cutting my hair and trimming my long white beard in the winter. Everything I do has purpose and functionality and most of all everything is real!

Everyone's "bucket list" should include: writing a book to help motivate and inspire people, building at least one home, try to semi-retire early enough in life to enjoy their free time and interests (besides semi-retirement is much better than full retirement because you can do it earlier in life and have more life left in you, this allows you to "stay in the game" longer to do the other things in life you enjoy). I also recommend living at least 10 years in the urban/suburban areas and 10 years in rural America before making your final decision on where to live the rest of your days. Who knows you may even want to move to a different place every few years after you "got your fill" from your last place. Variety!

It's very obvious, using real-life examples, that tolerance and equality have been a misused, semantic, delusional agenda driven propaganda by the "powers that be". We are long overdue as a country regarding the misuse of "victim/protectionist group" status. Just look at the lifestyles of the proponents of this obsolete system. Look at the Sharpton's and Jackson's lifestyle, lavish and extremely non-humbling. I believe the young congressman Jackson was recently indicted for stealing campaign money. When any group of people feel they have the right to be exempt from any of our rules, laws and accountability, it does them and the American people absolutely no good. The "powers that be" have made facts and reality politically incorrect and "virtual" reality the norm. They are dependent on "paper" investments, power and control like the common meth addict on the street.

I wish that my health was better so I can do all the things I used to love to do. I do miss going to the gym and lifting weights, hand splitting firewood, riding a motorcycle and wearing a heavy pack while hiking deep in the backwoods. Unfortunately, lots of that stuff is now filed away in my past memory. But, at least I have a lot of great memories regarding my physical adventures. I still try and hunt and fish with moderation and modifications as I mentioned earlier in this book, but I look at the glass half full every day and I am grateful for what I can do. One of my favorite examples to use is today's modern compound bow and arrow. Today's technology has "kept me in the game".......... and I am very grateful! I remember doing 100 push-ups at one time with ease. Well, I am building myself up these days and for the first time in over 10 years I can now do six push-ups. (I remember when I couldn't do any because my nerve damage and muscular atrophy was so compromising and my hands would shake uncontrollably). This is a huge break-through for me and I feel very blessed!

In summary, with so much corruption and phoney data broadcasting regularly by the agenda-driven "old media", we can clearly see the unfortunate direction America is heading. The elite's manipulation that is occurring financially, economically, socially and politically has made too many things artificial and uncertain. People don't even know what to believe anymore and, if they do believe, they are afraid to say anything. So much has lost value that would benefit our middle class today, yet at the same time, too many options are getting so expensive and out of reach for them as well. We might go into another war soon and we can't even take care of our existing combat veterans but, we can pay for millions of illegal aliens. (By the way, who goes to war for the big talkers and button pushers-the middle class and the poor, that's who)! How can the "powers that be" give such high salary's and pensions to government workers and practically ignore our combat veterans? How can they bankrupt our private sector middle class and give so much to the government sector.......and print so much money at the same time? 55% of our "workers" are government, do you think this is by design? So what should be the game plan for the middle class to control just a little more of their own destiny? Options are dwindling.

Maybe, if just some of the 90% of people who live in urban/suburban America, moved out into the country and developed new skills we as a country would be better prepared for most things that come our way. Skills that built America and that could easily dovetail with today's technology. Skills so they can re-claim their lives. We rarely even have to go shopping anymore because all we need can now be purchased on the internet. Plus, they ship anywhere! You don't even need a hard line phone anymore because anyone can get satellite internet.

We could get back to helping others, getting healthier and become more self-sufficient. We could have discussions about tangible in lieu of paper investments. The word manipulation of any context by the "powers that be" could be irrelevant. We could create more synergy and less division and not be known for what group we are in but, our hard work, results and helping others. We could communicate better, share ideas and strengthen communities. We could vote on-line for individual issues vs. wasting trillions of dollars for advertising on some bum who gets sent over to Washington to not honor his/her word. We could forget about Democrats or Republicans and start a "middle class" party of the people. We could start state and county run banks backed by tangible silver/gold and land.

We could bring back some manufacturing and real jobs. We could loosen some regulations, abolish the IRS, "outsource" our attorneys overseas and become more creative. We could, together, draw a line in the sand and say "no more" to political correctness. We could make decisions based on trust, respect, word of honor and truth. We could once again become free!

One of the greenhouses (All vegetables shown in my greenhouses are at least 6 ft high)

Some of the raised beds

Another greenhouse

Asparagus patch

One of my
greenhouses

Raspberry
patch

Solarium in action (young veggie plants before their garden debut).

Karen with elderberrys to make wine

Just two days of garden harvesting

Trail Cameras

Black Bear on my property

3 mountain lions on my property

Red Fox on my property

Whitetail doe and fawn on my property

Moose on my property

Bald Eagle on lion kill on my property

Grizzly harvested in Alaska

A nice elk

Mountain goat

26 inch rainbow trout caught on my property

60 pound beaver harvested on the Bitterroot River

Karen harvested this nice spring gobbler on the hobby farm this year. I contributed by calling it in.

Black bear harvested on my property

Harvested a whitetail buck on my property

Bighorn sheep harvested in central Montana

Otter
trapped
on my
property

Wolf trapped

Karen harvest-
ed a nice size
cow elk in the
valley

Mountain lion

Bobcat trapped

33inch Bull Trout caught on my property

Goat milking station I made for Karen

Karen with some of the farm crew

Karen making goat cheese w/ wood cook stove in background

Dutch oven
cooking

Solar oven
cooking

Hybrid cobb rocket
stove
(Look up rocket
stoves on the inter-
net. You can make
them yourself, for
indoors also, and use
only about 1/3 of the
firewood you would
use compared to a
wood stove.)

Karen and I, our
harvest of mushroom
picking

I took my Dad on a guided fishing trip on Flathead Lake. He caught two
19 pound Lake trout back to back. I got one of them mounted for him as a
present.

CPSIA information can be obtained at www.ICGtesting.com
Printed in the USA
BVOW11s0444130114

341458BV00009B/27/P